The
Jaguar Companion

Bringing home the Le Mans victors of the 1957 Le Mans. Ron Flockhart drives No. 3, with Ivor Bueb. W. E. 'Wilkie' Wilkinson (*centre*)

Photo: A. Dickson McLaren

The
Jaguar Companion

KENNETH ULLYETT

STANLEY PAUL
London

STANLEY PAUL & CO. LTD
178–202 Great Portland Street, London, W.1

AN IMPRINT OF THE   HUTCHINSON GROUP

London Melbourne Sydney
Auckland Bombay Toronto
Johannesburg New York

First published 1959
Second impression March 1960

*This book has been set in Baskerville type face. It has
been printed in Great Britain by The Anchor Press,
Ltd., in Tiptree, Essex, on Antique Wove paper and
bound by Taylor Garnett Evans & Co., Ltd., in
Watford, Herts*

ACKNOWLEDGMENTS

JAGUAR *is deservedly the subject of the first of the series of 'Companion Books', as by its achievements in racing, in competitions, and in every use throughout the world it has become the apothesis of the British-made sports car.*

This book is compiled, therefore, not only as a tribute to the vision, design and craftsmanship of the Jaguar team, but also to increase the pride of ownership whereby many thousands of Jaguar drivers the world over can learn the background to this famous marque *which has become part of the living history of motoring.*

This book will be of great interest to Jaguar drivers the world over, and it is not confined only to those cars sold in United Kingdom markets. There are many thousands of Jaguar drivers in the United States, for example, who are familiar not only with the routine XK120, XK140 and so on, but who have variants such as XK120 M, XK120 MC, XK140 M and others. Mechanical details of these cars are included in the following text, so this is the first complete Jaguar Companion available for American readers.

In the compilation of this book I am indebted to a very large number of people, official bodies, and private organizations, in particular the following: Mr. George Abecassis, D.F.C.; Barwell Motors Ltd. (Mr. Ronald Golding); Borg-Warner Ltd.; Carburettors Limited; Dunlop Rubber Co. Ltd. (Mr. Graham Parkes); Mr. J. Duncan Hamilton, F.R.Ae.S.; Jaguar Drivers' Club (Mr. Eric G. Brown); Mr. Brian Lister; Joseph Lucas Ltd.; Measham Publications Ltd. (Mr. Claude A. Page); Merchiston Motors (Mr. David Murray, C.A., and Mr. W. E. Wilkinson); Mr. Stirling Moss; Mr. Georges Roesch, M.I.Mech.E.; the Royal Automobile Club; the Royal Society of Arts; Shorrock Superchargers Ltd. (Miss Kathleen Humphrey); Solex Ltd. (Mr. C. J. Findlay); Mr. J. M. Tojeiro; Tourist Trophy Garage Ltd.

Finally, I am greatly indebted to a number of Jaguar experts who by their discussions with me through the years inspired this book, and who themselves have left a proud memory of their achievements in automobile engineering in general and with Jaguar in particular—notably the late Mike Hawthorn, Geoffrey Smith, and R. M. V. Sutton.

KENNETH ULLYETT

THE ROYAL AUTOMOBILE CLUB

CONTENTS

CONTENTS

ILLUSTRATIONS

Illustrations

FOREWORD

by STIRLING MOSS

If any proof were needed that racing improves the breed, and that stamina and the automobile equivalent of 'bloodstock' are developed by contests such as a Grand Prix d'Endurance, then surely Jaguar is convincing proof?

Of course a large number of very good motor-cars are produced by manufacturers who do not subject their cars to a twenty-four-hour marathon such as Le Mans, but in the interests of national prestige as well as of mechanical development it is obviously a very good thing that a number of leading manufacturers like Jaguar have, in turn, entered in these great national contests.

The result is many-sided. On the one hand, Jaguar have obviously made a big dent in the bonnet of Continental racing supremacy. And on the other, the expert can see many detail features in chassis design which come from continued experience in racing.

I must say I am very glad this book has been written, because it will enable owners of Jaguars, owners of other fine cars, and perhaps owners of no car at all, to appreciate and enjoy the exciting story of this very famous make. History is often rather dull stuff, but not, I think, when it comes to any branch of motor sport.

Of course I personally enjoy reading again the accounts of how I was privileged to be invited to join the Jaguar Works Team, how we tried out disc brakes and other then-top-secret chassis and engine features under actual racing conditions. In 1951, when I first drove a Jaguar on the Le Mans circuit, it is now a matter of history that they won the race at 93·4 m.p.h., and two years later they did it again, breaking every record for speed and distance, taking 1st, 2nd, 4th and 9th places, to give Britain her greatest Le Mans victory of all time—even more glorious than the old pre-war days when Bentley 'wore the green'.

In THE JAGUAR COMPANION Kenneth Ullyett tells much more than racing stories, of course. He has talked with the engineers, mechanics, and experts of oil, fuel, tyre and accessory companies who have contributed to Jaguar success; so this book includes a great deal of technical and servicing information from private sources, and I am quite sure will prove invaluable to the private owner who wants to ensure continuing reliability, and perhaps to get some increased performance as well.

The sole comment I feel bound to make on one very instructive chapter, which describes how some experts get extra 'urge' from their engines, is that I hope it does not tempt you to regard your sports-tourer as a Grand Prix racer, nor to use the public highways as a race-track! The cautious driver will benefit, I am sure, from the information given here, as safe driving frequently demands a good standard of acceleration and rapid braking.

In these pages you will find that Kenneth Ullyett has included numerous accounts of the trials and developments of a number of features such as petrol-injection, disc brakes and special tyres which are in a sense an integral part of the Jaguar theme. That is why I am glad of the opportunity of writing this Foreword and of welcoming this book which sets on record the salient facts of a fine British *marque*.

One

SETTING THE PACE...

ON A misty London November evening in 1954, two
strangely contrasted men were received in the beautiful
Adelphi building which the Adams brothers erected in 1774
for the Royal Society of Arts, and which has been occupied by
that learned Society ever since.

The distinguished visitors were Sir William Lyons, chairman of Jaguar Cars Limited, and Signor Pinin Farina the
eminent Italian designer, and they were received by Sir
Francis Meynell, the Master of the Faculty of Royal Designers
for Industry. The Council of the Royal Society of Arts confers
on outstanding designers the distinction of Royal Designer for
Industry, the highest to be obtained in the field of industrial
art. It may at no time be held by more than forty recipients,
and a small number of non-British designers are made Honor-
ary holders of the distinction.

We gathered in the Society's historic 'Great Room' as Sir
Francis introduced the two new members of the Faculty to us.
Of Sir William (then Mr.) Lyons, he said: 'He is a recent Past
President of the Society of Motor Manufacturers and Traders,
and he has produced outstanding cars, and produces them at
remarkably low prices, which have won fame for this country
throughout the world. And he has not subjected himself to
American trends—he has really influenced American trends.

'He has managed to penetrate what I may call the "Chro-
mium Curtain" of the United States. His car is a *sine qua non*
for the heroes of American films, and in the best novels a really
smart and luxurious man of the world is sure to have a Jaguar.
... But seriously, he is not merely a brilliant *entrepreneur*. He has
himself worked at the drawing-board in every phase of motor-
car design. His car, of course—as he is eager to declare—is the

13

result of teamwork. But he is the captain, and not merely the captain: he is the No. 1 all-rounder.

'Some cars are made to look as if they are going fast even when they are stock still. That, I suppose, is an art. Other cars are made to look stable when they are going very, very fast. That is the art—the better art—of Lyons' Jaguar. . . .'

As this paean rang around the historic room, I recalled how Sir William himself had always placed the emphasis on the importance of design and planning. The Jaguar success is no accident.

'I think that of all the problems a car manufacturer has to face, the planning of a new model is the most difficult,' he said at the time he was President of the S.M.M. & T. 'The root of the problem is that, no matter in what form a new model is presented by a manufacturer, if it fails to meet with public favour then neither the efficiency of his manufacturing organization nor the competency of his world sales organization can save him from a situation verging on disaster. . . .'

In the past decade a number of sections of the motor industry have found themselves on the verge of such a situation; but during that same period Jaguar has achieved success in every field. Sir William, 'the captain, the No. 1 all-rounder', must be proud of what his team has achieved.

Financially, Jaguar Cars Ltd. is the envy of many other sections of the industry. In March 1959 it was on record that the company had made a net profit of £624,337 for the year, that 17½ per cent was being paid on Ordinary shares, that of all Jaguar cars produced 54 per cent were exported, and that the American and Canadian subsidiary companies had reached a record-breaking total of $22,000,000.

In the world of international motor sport Sir William could reflect with pride that since the marathon of Le Mans first came into existence in 1906, as the A.C. de la Sarthe, this gruelling 24-hour event had been a victory for Britain eleven glorious times—five by Jaguar, five by Bentley and once by Lagonda. The fastest Le Mans in 1957 was a victory for Ron Flockhart and Ivor Bueb (of the famous privately owned Scottish racing team Ecurie Ecosse), who averaged 113·85 m.p.h. during their total of 2,732 miles covered in the twenty-four hours.

Sir William himself said: 'Although our decision, made in 1956, to withdraw from official participation in racing and other competitive events has been maintained, this has by no means resulted in the disappearance of the name of Jaguar from the lists of winners in track and road events. . . . The Lister Engineering Company continue to use our engines for their highly successful Lister-Jaguar racing cars. These cars won no less than six important national and international races in Europe last year (1958), and seven events in America, where Jaguar driver Walter Hansgen won the Sports Car Club of America Championship for the second year in succession.

'Of the many successes gained by private owners, the most recent was the winning of the Nominated Team Prize in the Monte Carlo Rally (1959) by three privately owned and entered 3·4-litre Jaguars. . . . In another field of sport Mr. Norman Buckley set up a new one-hour water speed record for 800-kilogramme boats with his Jaguar-engined *Miss Windermere III*, which attained the speed of 89·08 m.p.h.'

Jaguar has indeed become much more than a car *marque*. It is today a symbol, a way of life. Famous (and the infamous) sit at the wheel. V.I.P.s headed by royalty drive Jaguars. Queen Ingrid of Denmark has a new 115-m.p.h. Mk. IX saloon, her third Jaguar in a row. The Duke of Kent drives a red Jaguar XK. Officialdom has turned from stately limousines to Jaguars for national functions. A team of official Jaguars paraded the Preston By-pass, Britain's first motorway, at its opening ceremony.

In life, as well as in life seen through the eyes of novelists and scenario-writers, the Jaguar has become a symbol of twentieth-century gracious luxury. The celebrated live—and sometimes, regrettably, die—in them. Like Rolls-Royce, the name Jaguar has become accepted as a standard of luxury, integrity and downright opulence by millions to whom the prospect of owning either is an impossible dream.

It is therefore strange to recall that the original dream of Sir William Lyons, as a youngster of twenty-one, was to provide inexpensive but good-quality transport for the middle-classes, in particular for motor-cyclists wanting to take their family in a sidecar.

Lyons, born on 4th September 1901, in Blackpool, went to

Arnold House (today the Arnold School), Blackpool, and like many other youngsters became caught up in the cycling and motor-cycling boom of the immediate post-war years, when motoring was only for the wealthy, and the cycle-car movement was struggling with vehicles such as the B.S.A., Belsize-Bradshaw, A.B.C., A.V. Monocar, Rollo and others based on primitive aircraft design and a great deal of unfounded optimism.

At the height of this period, in 1922, I recall a visit to the Olympia Motor-Cycle Show, where young Lyons and his partner Bill Walmsley were exhibiting their first sidecar. On Stand No. 180 were two examples of the sidecars made by the newly formed Swallow Side Car Co. (later 'The Swallow Side Car and Coachbuilding Co.') whose premises were a small workshop in Bloomfield Road, Blackpool.

Lyons already had considerable motor-cycling experience, and he knew that the sidecars of that period lacked many important features. Some were too flimsily made, had no coach finish, or were too heavy for the 350 c.c. and 500 c.c. machines to which the 'chairs' were fitted. Lyons, Walmsley and their small staff of three men and a boy produced two Exhibition sidecars in time for the Olympia show. One weighed 80lb., and was suitable for machines up to 2¾ h.p. The price was £21 10s., including Triplex screen and coverall apron. The larger 'chair' shown was for machines up to 8-h.p. twins, and weighed about 100 lb. It had a bulbous back, and was built up in eight panels with internal ribs and a nose of steel. Side and bottom ribs were of straight-grain ash, while mouldings were of canary-wood. The production of such an ambitious sidecar was a sign that the workmen in Bloomfield Street knew their craft of coachbuilding. Lyons recruited the foreman from a firm who made carriages, while another man had aircraft experience.

'Lamps adaptable either to electricity or acetylene,' ran the small sign on Stand No. 180, which also stated that the price of this super-luxurious 'chair' was £30 complete (lamps extra).

The Motor Cycle recorded: 'Both models are of very sound and workmanlike appearance. . . .' *Motor-Cycling* (29th November 1922), however, carried an editorial opinion which must have been weighing very much on young Lyons' mind as he walked around Olympia, looking at his rivals' products.

The classic XK—the 3½-litre XK120 super-sports two-seater as first introduced a decade ago. This original version clocked 132·6 m.p.h. on the
Jabbeke-Aeltre Road circuit, on 30th May 1949, the highest speed then
attained with a standard car run on ordinary petrol

Prototype Dunlop disc brakes being tested on the Fort Dunlop skid-pan, with a
works Jaguar Mk. VII. An XK140 was also used in the initial tests while the
brakes were being perfected by the Dunlop team of Mr. H. J. Butler (Design),
H. Hodkinson and A. J. Holloway (Development)

One of the finest examples of British automobile engineering development, the classic XK engine. This near-side view clearly shows the twin S.U. carburetter layout and the polished casing of the two-stage duplex roller-chain drive of the 70-degree twin camshafts. Capacity is 3,442 c.c. (83 mm. bore and 106 mm. stroke), developing 160 b.h.p. at 5,000 r.p.m.

'It can be unreservedly claimed,' they wrote, 'that no show of recent years could equal in interest that which opened at Olympia on Saturday last. . . . While we do not agree for one moment with those pessimists who persist in foretelling the extermination of the sidecar by the cheap light car, we cannot but think that it is unfortunate that the Car Show precedes the Motor-cycle Exhibition.

Many a buyer has visited the Car Show and has been mesmerized by the external attractiveness of some of the light cars into forgetting their comparatively poor value considered with the higher-grade motor-cycles. . . . The extraordinary value presented by some of the bigger passenger motor-cycle combinations would have convinced waverers that the sidecar has considerably strengthened its position as the best value for money. . . .'

Now value for money is something which is for ever occupying the mind of every Blackpool *entrepreneur*, and when Lyons saw the miniature Seven which Sir Herbert Austin produced in time for the same Show of 1922, he realized that at a list price of £225 it was going to bring motoring—real motoring, not wet and draughty motor-cycling—to a new public of millions.

Lyons became known to the team who had devised this magic Seven for which Sir Herbert is often given the sole credit, namely his brother Harry Austin (responsible for chassis production at Longbridge), Mr. H. Challoner the Austin coachbuilding expert, and Mr. A. J. Hancock, a draughtsman who had been the first to join Austin in 1905 when the Austin Motor Company was born.

It is now a matter of history that the little car was an instant success, despite the rather pram-like appearance of the earlier models. A. C. R. Waite, who had raced the Austin Twenty, began to clock up Brooklands and other records with a sports version of the Seven, and the impact of the first real midget car was such that by 1926 the Austin factory was extended to 62 acres, about 8,000 workers were producing nearly 25,000 Austin Sevens a year, and within the first three years of the car's introduction sales were amounting to some £3,900,000 annually for the home market and £875,000 for export.

Just as Henry Ford brought motoring to the millions with

the Model-T, so Sir Herbert Austin helped to change the social pattern of the nation with the first 'big car in miniature'.

Minor changes were made in engine auxiliaries, and major changes made in the chassis and coachwork; but the engine remained basically unaltered for fourteen years. Electric starting was incorporated in 1924, and coil ignition adopted in 1929. A three-bearing crankshaft was introduced in 1936. The first Seven had a bore and stroke of 54 by 76·2 mm. (giving 698 c.c.), but within the first year the bore was increased to 56 mm., giving a capacity of 747·5 c.c. The weight of the original 'pram' tourer was just over 6½ cwt., but with the larger-bore engine the total weight for the standard coachwork went up to 8 cwt.

Gordon England Cup Models and a few minor variants became popular, especially when the Murray Jamieson racer appeared at Brooklands, and when in the hands of Kay Petre, Hadley and Goodacre the racing Austin became the fastest car in its class prior to the Second World War. Only one design-feature of the Seven handicapped it for those builders of specials and de-luxe coachwork who wanted to turn the Austin car-for-the-millions into something more classy. It was that the stumpy frame stopped short at the back, close to the spring anchorage, thus putting a heavy load on the body-sill. This limitation of chassis design was a great handicap to coachbuilders. Gordon England, with the fabric-covered Cup Model, overcame the difficulty by having a two-seater with virtually no back-end at all.

Lyons and Walmsley applied their sidecar-construction technique to this new problem. The Austin frame was strengthened, and triangulation enabled the team in Blackpool to fit a body which was virtually a big sports saloon in miniature to the chassis which had parallel characteristics.

Longbridge mass-production was already cutting the price of the standard Seven (reduced by 1930 to £130), but the comparatively small overheads of Lyons' team enabled him to list the Swallow Austin, with de-luxe equipment, at only £187. Space for car-body production was found in a works in Cocker Street, Blackpool, and this classic Swallow version took its place in the long and successful evolution of the Seven. To Lyons and Walmsley it was the major turning-point. For the first time, they were in the car business. . . .

Early versions of the Swallow Austin coupé had a hinged head to facilitate entry, but the domed-roof design was introduced, with a sports-type V screen, giving rather more internal space. The hinged coupé was still continued, however, with a two-bolt fixing at the rear and a clip on the windscreen rail. Alternatively a folding hood could be fitted. The open sports model sold at £175, while the list price of the coupé with hood was £190; all good value, with quality, in the mid-twenties.

'Pa' Austin took a liking to the keen young coachbuilder from Blackpool, and as A. V. Davidge and other associates of Sir Herbert were building up sales of the Seven at a fantastic rate, the chance was eagerly grasped to deliver as many chassis as Lyons could handle.

Here an embarrassing impasse arose, for Lyons had arranged to take chassis in batches of fifty, this being as much as family funds and the slender resources of the Swallow company could tolerate; and he felt that if he cut the order, Sir Herbert—whose loyal stubbornness was equalled by his irascibility—might cancel it completely. To make matters worse, the Cocker Street team could produce no more than twelve bodies a week without increasing staff, works-space and plant. Such an increase meant bigger capital outlay, and less cash available for purchase of chassis from Longbridge! However, Lyons was not the first budding automotive tycoon to find himself the anxious focal point of such an unhappy circle of circumstances.

The difficulty was eased quickly by ingenuity, and by good fortune. The ingenuity was exemplified by a straight talk with the stationmaster at Blackpool Central, who was asked to be a little tolerant when Austin Seven chassis were piled in the sidings and could not be removed to Cocker Street for some days. The good fortune, deservedly, came from increased sales, which provided extra working capital. At Cocker Street Lyons installed flow-production-in-miniature methods, and soon production was stepped up to nearly fifty bodies a week.

Extra jigs and tools were made to handle similar Swallow bodies for other chassis. From 1923 to 1928 the familar Swallow sports saloon was found on Swift, Wolseley Hornet, Fiat and, of course, Standard. It is interesting in retrospect to recall why these Swallow designs were such good sellers.

There was a growing public who revolted against anything

that looked like mass-production, but who nevertheless could afford no more than 25 per cent above average list price for something exclusive. Secondly, Lyons coachwork was beautifully designed and finished, and the rounded Swallow lines appealed to the motorist and his wife, who probably felt (as Sir Francis Meynell said thirty years later) that here was a car 'made to look as if it were going very fast when standing stock still'. Well, there certainly was a charm in semi-streamlining, V-screens and the rounded rear-quarters of this diminutive luxury saloon, particularly in an age when so many other car bodies resembled baths, prams or horse-drawn carriages.

In addition, Lyons—inheriting, perhaps, a dash of the Blackpool showman—was one of the first coachwork designers to appreciate the sales-virtue of colour. Most standard tourers were black, navy or maroon. Cream was reserved almost entirely for the wire spokes of semi-sports cars. Lyons introduced an attractive two-colour scheme for the Swallow-Austin. The first version was cream with crimson-lake. Later an alternative was listed, grey, with green wings, chassis and top. These became very typical two-colour schemes of the late-1920's period, but it was Lyons who first introduced them.

A probably unforeseen second turning-point was when he first met Captain (later Sir) John Black of Standards, to discuss a coachbuilding proposition on similar lines to that established with 'Pa' Austin.

The Standard Company was founded at the turn of the century by the late R. H. Maudsley to build cars on a then-new 'standard' basis, at a time when most others were still individually hand-made. This standard production schedule gave the firm its name. For many years the high quality of Standards (in particular the reliability and longevity of the light 11-h.p. car, with exposed overhead valve gear) ranked their products equal with Charron-Laycock and similar high-grade designs of the early 'twenties, but the company suffered vicissitudes during the post-war industrial depression, and eventually, when the £300,000 company was showing a £150,000 loss, Captain J. P. Black—at thirty-five a dynamic organizer and engineer—was brought in to help put things right.

He has always shunned personal publicity, and today, farming in retirement at Llanbedr, Merioneth, after holding the deputy-chairmanship of an electrical group, has for personal reasons cut himself away from the automobile industry for which he helped to create one of the 'Big Six'. In retrospect, however, Black has never been given the credit due to him for his bold pioneering at a time when other motor firms went under. Nor did he have a free hand at Standards through the years. Outspoken, brusque in his Army manner, challenging and not afraid to create angry critics, Black held most of the reins, but not all. At various periods of Standard history other executives such as Charles Band were titular heads of the company, and it was rumoured that many of Black's projects (some of which indirectly and probably unwittingly helped to form the fortunes of Jaguar) were carried through against bitter opposition.

When Black took over in 1928, the Standard Motor Company listed three main models, the Nine (actual R.A.C. rating 8·9 h.p.), the '14–28' (13·9 h.p.) and the '18–36' (17·4 h.p.). The Nine had a side-valve engine, and the other two models used o.h.v. units. All three chassis had worm-drive transmission.

Apart from making essential financial cuts, streamlining production and installing new plant, Black's first bold plan was to concentrate on the Nine, with an entirely revised version. Owing to the depression, culminating in the General Strike, the greatest chance of expansion—or, indeed, of survival—lay in the light-car field which had already given Austin and Morris their golden opportunity. Black then concentrated on the rugged Sixteen, today generally agreed to be one of the soundest Standard designs.

This is the period, of course, at which Black and Lyons made their important agreement resulting in the first 'S.S.', but because of the present-day international ramifications of Standards it is interesting to see how the pattern of the Standard story subsequently developed. The series of Flying Standards in the mid-'thirties, using the firm's old-established Union Jack motif (it had long been an emblem used in the design of the radiator badge), brought Black into direct competition with Austin and Morris, and towards the close of the Flying Standard era Black's energies were also devoted to a Top Secret mission in the national interest—the creation of 'shadow' factories. Subsequently in 1943 he was knighted as some token of reward for his work as head of the shadow-factory scheme.

During the war Mosquito aircraft were built in Standard's own shadow factories, and Black and his new young personal assistant Alick Dick (today the company's managing director) were contemplating car production plans to commence as soon as possible after D-Day. With Charles Band as head of the company, Sir John Black carried through a bold one-model policy. No more 'Little Nines' and 'Big Sixteens'. Standard concentrated on the Vanguard, which was one of Britain's first true post-war designs in the Detroit body-style. The Vanguard had the classic 2,088 c.c. four-cylinder push-rod o.h.v. engine rated at 17·9 h.p., developing 68 b.h.p. at 4,200 r.p.m., which so impressed millionaire Harry Ferguson that it formed the basis of the mammoth deal whereby Ferguson tractors used Vanguard engines. (In later years, Standards spent £4,500,000 on machine tools for the Massey-Harris-Ferguson TR35 tractor.)

Continuing his amazing industrial career, Sir John Black bought up Triumph, revolutionized Coventry pay-scales with an incentive bonus and then automation, and in 1949 became the storm centre of political controversy when the Standard Company awarded him a tax-free gift of nearly £100,000 worth of shares. This was such an embarrassment to the Socialist Government that Sir Stafford Cripps sought legislation whereby the gift was taxed, retrospectively, and thus rendered almost worthless to Sir John.

In 1953 he was involved in a serious car smash, and as a result of a family bereavement there were rumours of his impending retirement. He returned to Standards, however, to replace Charles Band as chairman, and then for personal reasons decided after all that he would retire. Alick Dick was already appointed to a senior position, and Marshal of the Royal Air Force Lord Tedder was in the chair, despite criticism in some quarters of a Service chief in such a post. Standards awarded him £30,000 (this time taking fresh legal advice to ensure that it really would be tax-free), and Sir John Black—with a mixed bag of memories, some proud and some poignant, from his long career in the industry—handed over to Lord Tedder and thirty-six-year-old Alick Dick an organization producing around 98,000 cars and 70,000 tractors, employing nearly 15,000 people, and making a profit (before taxation) of over £3,000,000 annually.

This, then, is the brusque, dynamic giant with whom William Lyons first contacted when the project was mooted for a Swallow Standard. He was not, of course, the only man to suggest a body-building proposition to Captain Black, for Jensen of Birmingham was also developing a sports two-seater based on a Standard Nine chassis. *The Autocar* of 24th May 1929 gave a description of young Jensen's sports Standard, at that time unnamed but referred to as 'a 9-h.p. Standard altered to suit the owner's ideas'. It had smart lines, a V-shaped radiator, cycle-type front wings, louvred cover for the dumb-irons, alloy castings giving the appearance of a knock-off Rudge hubcap, and general flowing lines creating the impression of a 'Brooklands' model.

By October 1929 The New Avon Body Company of Warwick accepted the Jensen design as a sequel to their own special coachwork for the Triumph Super Seven (£75 for the fabric-covered sports saloon), and the Jensen thus became the Avon Standard, with stone-guard for the V-radiator, valance, and boat tail. The spare wheel was strapped to the driver's side of the body in true sporting style, and the same mock-Rudge hub-caps were fitted. This not unattractive little car, in its standard Avon blue finish, was listed at £250, and for a while was a competitor with the Swallow Standard—a circumstance which probably gives Jensen (with his present ultra-modern and successful 541 R, disc-braked all round) a wry smile of nostalgia nowadays.

Production of the Swallow versions of the Austin, Standard and Hornet were straining the capacity of the Cocker Street team, and now Lyons was anxious to be in Coventry, in the very heart of the industry. He was twenty-seven, ambitious, popular, deservedly successful. And he had plans for his own car, not merely for building sporting coachwork on other men's chassis.

In 1928 Walmsley and Lyons decided to move to Coventry. At first they only rented a small bay in a former shell-filling factory—a munitions depot of the First World War later used by a number of small Coventry manufacturers.

Jigs and tools and stock from Cocker Street were transported in wooden crates to the new bay at Foleshill, and a few months later, when Swallow Austins and Swallow Standards were coming regularly off the lines from this more central address, Lyons ventured to discuss with Black the proposition for a new sports car, and Frank Hough of Henly's liked the design and agreed to back it with his huge sales organization.

Over the old brick building a strip of bold white lettering was painted:

SWALLOW SIDE CAR COMPANY : : MANUFACTURERS
OF SIDE CARS & LIGHT CAR BODIES : : COACH
PAINTERS AND TRIMMERS

Now Lyons could visualize a complete break with the past, and the production of a car which would tally with his own ideals as nearly as the needs of commercial marketing permitted. Delightful but usually improbable stories are told of the various meetings between young Lyons and Captain Black, who was indeed only ten years his senior.

It is usually believed (although the story is denied by Sir John Black) that Lyons suggested the initials 'S.S.' for the new model, as an abbreviation for 'Swallow Sports'. Black, however, took this to be an abbreviation for 'Sports Standard', or perhaps for 'Standard Swallow', and agreed. Neither could possibly foresee that within seven years the same initials, applied to Hitler's Storm Troopers, would be among the most-loathed and feared letters in the newspaper alphabet.

If in truth there ever was any difference of opinion between Lyons and Black on this little detail, there was certainly complete agreement on major policy. Black agreed to provide versions of the Big Nine and the Sixteen chassis, modified to suit Lyons' instructions, based on a design mutually agreed with Bill Walmsley.

A Henly advertisement in the national motoring Press at the end of July 1931 read:

WAIT! . . . *The 'S.S.' is Coming.* Two New Coupés of Surpassing Beauty. S.S. is the name of a new car that is going to thrill the hearts of the motoring public and the trade alike. It is something utterly new . . . different . . .

better! Long . . . low . . . very low . . . and very FAST. At
the Show, or before, two S.S. Coupés of surpassing beauty
will be presented. WAIT . . . THE S.S. IS COMING. . . .

In this fashion the car that was 'utterly new, different', was
heralded to the public. Noël Coward could not have written
better advertising copy. Everyone was 'utterly' happy, except
perhaps the stock clerk who pointed out that considerable
stocks of the Swallow Standard still stood in the Foleshill bay,
for trade rumours were circulating about a new model—always
a bad way of selling an existing one. So, in a last-minute amend-
ment, Henly's announced that: 'The extremely successful
Standard Swallow 4-seater saloons to be continued. Big Nine
Saloon £250. . . .'

On the design of the new car, Lyons took the advice of
many expert friends. The late Geoffrey Smith, managing
editor of *The Autocar*, was among the fortunate circle privileged
to discuss certain features of the new car with Lyons, and one
day (just before the production of the Airline, which was a subsequent development of the S.S.) Lyons swung round in his
leather office chair and faced the genial Smith with a blunt:
'You know, I'm going to put chairs like *these* in my new car.
Why should a man have to tolerate worse seating comfort in
his car than he has in his own office? . . .'

And, for the Airline, Lyons saw to it that the seats were
indeed modelled on the deep leather armchairs in his office.

The versions of the S.S. (the Sixteen, followed by the Nine)
were of course based on Standard chassis, but modifications
were so extensive that Coventry was startled out of its rut.

'For many years, Swallow coachwork on popular cars
has had a distinctive appearance,' commented *The Autocar*
in October 1931, on the birth of the S.S. 'Light sporting
coachwork with attractive colour-schemes for the Austin
Seven, Standard and Wolseley Hornet Sports have been
acclaimed by many as *the best-looking cars yet produced*. Now
the S.S. coupé startles the country anew—the first car to
have its chassis designed by the bodybuilder.'

Indeed, the changes were fundamental, and were associated
with every car that Lyons produced subsequently for many

years. The frame was of the double-dropped type, the side-members at the front parallel from the dumb-irons as far as the cross-members beneath the radiator, then a V-taper to a point about two-thirds of the way along the engine-length, and finally parallel to the rear dumb-irons. The frame was downswept by the gearbox, swept up over the rear axle, and the frame was very strong, having channel and tubular cross-members, and tubular tie-rods between both dumb-irons. In past years Lyons had suffered from badly braced chassis to which some of his coachwork was fitted; now, as designer of his own car, he knew that a very strong frame was the foundation of a successful vehicle.

To achieve the 'low—VERY low' lines announced by Henly's, the long, flat, half-elliptic springs (with nine leaves) were fitted outside the frame, not under it. Wheelbase of the S.S.1 was 9 ft. 4 in., three inches longer than the Standard Sixteen, and also about one inch wider at the rear. While the front and rear axles were Standard components, they were modified to take genuine Rudge knock-off caps, with racing-type wheels fitted with 550 × 18 Dunlop tyres. The axle ratio was stepped up to give 4·66 : 1 in place of the standard 5·11 : 1, resulting in an overall 6·15 : 1 top-gear ratio. The steering was sharply raked, of course, and Marles-Weller cam-and-lever steering was used.

The Standard Sixteen engine was set some seven inches further back in the frame. This engine was of 2,054 c.c. capacity (65·5 × 102 mm.), with the six cylinders cast in one with the top half of the crankcase. The exceptionally rigid crankshaft was carried in seven main bearings of 2-in. diameter. Aluminium pistons with duralumin connecting-rods were used. Engine accessories were of top quality, and in a number of detail points such as the oil-level indicator, which was of the float type, not dipstick, Rolls-Royce practice was followed.

Several important modifications were made to the Standard single-plate dry clutch and four-speed gearbox, cast aluminium extensions being used to carry the selector rods.

Coachwork was of course of the now well-established Swallow quality, with large seats of genuine Vaumol leather. The underslung frame resulted in an overall height for the S.S.1 coupé of 4 ft. 8 in. The appearance of the coupé, with its helmet-type semi-cycle wings in front (later changed to swept wings and sports running-boards) was startling, judged by 1931 standards. Three could be accommodated in the front (the centre passenger being slightly hampered by the central sports-type stumpy gear-lever and the fly-off handbrake), and there was room for two children or one adult in the rear seat. Even more startling than the appearance was the price—£325. A bid was made to list the S.S.1 at £310, but even in 1931 inflation was already rearing its head.

'Utterly unique,' said the Henly advertisements. 'Lower ... faster ... silent third ... flashing acceleration ... 60 ... 70 ... 75 m.p.h. ...'

Anything so startling immediately raised doubts as to whether it could possibly be as good as it looked, and still be sold at such a modest figure. Rumours began to circulate, but Lyons did not worry. There could be no hitch in deliveries of chassis, and he knew there would be no hold-up in the Foleshill works. He had but to wait until the motoring journalists and the public found the real worth of the car.

This they did. And subsequent minor changes to the S.S. design overcame early criticism. The Nine appeared in 1932, and now the Sixteen S.S.1 was being listed at £325, and the 20 h.p. version for £10 extra. As the S.S.11 was based on the Standard Little Nine, it was being listed with a four-speed box for £210. Wheelbase of the senior car was extended by seven inches, to give more coachwork space in the rear, and there were detail changes in the chassis frame. An armoured dash was incorporated, designed to exclude heat and fumes. Two armchair-type rear seats were now fitted. The revised S.S. used Lancegaye safely glass, Wilmot-Breeden chassis accessories, and was fitted with a Pytchley sliding roof.

In the summer of 1932 A. G. Douglas Clease, B.SC., was asked to pile up 1,000 miles in a single weekend on the 1933-type S.S.1. He described it as: 'A long, low, beautiful thing of graceful, sweeping lines.' For this long, fast weekend run, tyre pressures were kept at around 24 p.s.i., and advantage was taken of the new S.U. jet control to keep consumption figures down. Forty miles were covered in the very first hour's handling. Oil pressure settled down to a steady 30 p.s.i., and engine temperature was maintained at a steady 78°C. Douglas Clease enjoyed a fast climb up Shap, raced the L.M.S. Scots express, and with his foot hard down the speedometer needle swung to 80. He reached the Tarbet Hotel on Loch Lomond, having covered 330 miles in a day. The run through Glen Coe was made, by Loch Ness, and the Glen Doe climb with its 1 in 5 gradient. The engine did not boil. Over the crude roads then existing in the Mallaig area, with ruts and boulders, a 26-m.p.h. average was nevertheless maintained, and the car was returned to Birmingham after 1,054 trouble-free miles had been covered in four days. Douglas Clease reported that no fatigue was felt, largely owing to the precise steering and the rigidity of the underslung frame.

'Lyons achieved a new kind of design and production break-through by offering a combination of features not previously available,' said a U.S. motoring journalist. 'He gave daringly racey and beautiful lines, luxurious finish and fine workmanship, all at an astonishingly low price. It was Lyons' own rare combination of talents that made such an achievement possible. He is simultaneously a designer with a remarkable eye for line, an energetic production man with a flair for getting quantity and quality at low cost, a sales-man with an understanding of publicity techniques seldom found in British industry; a forceful, hard-headed business-man. . . .'

By 1933 the car-building and the sidecar plants were separated. The Swallow Side Car concern continued as a separate entity until 1939, while the Lyons and Walmsley interests in car construction were taken by S.S. Cars Ltd. Lyons was still only thirty-two years of age, on the threshold of achievement, and already beginning to realize the importance of teamwork.

In 1935 a pupil engineer and drawing-office designer from Humbers joined him, William Munger Heynes. That single event, possibly not so important at the time, proved to be the beginning of a new, golden era for all that William Lyons represented in the international motoring sphere.

Two

THE JAGUAR TEAM

A LARGE part of Jaguar success is inextricably bound up with the team who design, build, sell, drive and race. This last remains true even though the Jaguar company officially withdrew from racing at the close of the 1956 season.

Naturally the composition of these various teams has changed through the years, and some of the experts who worked with Sir William Lyons have gone on to rival organizations.

The success of the S.S.1 induced Lyons to develop a design team of his own, and in 1935 when the rumours in Coventry of a startlingly new S.S. were rife, one of the most promising designers was invited to join him. W. M. Heynes, M.I.MECH.E., M.S.A.E., born in Leamington Spa in 1903, had been educated at Warwick School and in 1922 became a pupil engineer with Humber Ltd. Completing his training in 1925, he worked in the Humber drawing office for the next four-and-a-half years, joining the Lyons team in 1935. He was appointed to the board in 1946, after the ground-work had been done on the Mk. V Jaguar.

Heynes is not the only member of the original team, however, for he was joined by Ernest William Rankin, a Londoner who entered the motor-car industry thirty-five years ago, and at one time was an advertising representative of a big American group. He was appointed Press officer to Lyons in 1934, and became a Council Member and a founder of the Coventry Publicity Association. The work he began for Jaguar is today being amplified by Mr. R. E. 'Bob' Berry, a popular figure with the world's motoring Press.

Another member of the team, none the less important even when Jaguar officially withdrew from racing, is Frank Raymond England, 'Lofty' as he is known to all racing enthusiasts.

Since 1956 he has been service director of Jaguar Cars Ltd., but he is no doubt better known to the outside world as the Jaguar racing chief.

'Lofty', a Christ College, Finchley, boy, was apprenticed to the Daimler Company at Hendon the year that Swallow's moved to Coventry, and ultimately he became racing mechanic to such great track figures as Sir Henry Birkin, Whitney Straight, Dick Seaman, B. Bira and to the E.R.A. organization. Between 1932 and 1938 'Lofty' was in action at most of the tracks in Europe, helping to 'soup' cars for extra speed and trackworthiness, and generally making sure that his team won. Alvis Ltd. managed to get his services in 1938 until the outbreak of war, when 'Lofty' flew with the R.A.F., returning to Alvis on the cessation of hostilities until eventually Lyons induced him to become Jaguar service manager. In 1951, when it became Lyons' policy to race official Jaguar teams, 'Lofty' was appointed competitions manager.

Behind the scenes 'Lofty' has assisted many who continued to fly the flag for Jaguar after the official withdrawal. As Sir William himself said, in explaining this withdrawal: 'It was felt in many quarters that this might well result in a break in the long run of successes our works cars had achieved for so many years all over the world, notably at Le Mans. So far from this being the case, the 1957 Le Mans resulted in privately owned and entered Jaguars achieving the most sweeping victory ever recorded by any make of car in this famous race. The final placings were Jaguar 1st, 2nd, 3rd, 4th and 6th, the first two places being gained by the Scottish Ecurie Ecosse team, the third place by a private French entry, the fourth place by a private Belgian entry and the sixth place by another British entry.' The background to much of this success, especially in the spheres of chassis preparation and the testing of disc brakes and other accessories for victory, is the work of 'Lofty' England.

One who was member of the original team is Walter Hassan, A.M.I.MECH.E., later Chief Engineer of Coventry Climax Engines Ltd. Hassan, four years Lyons' junior, was educated at the Northern Polytechnic and the Hackney Institute of Engineering. He joined Bentley Motors in 1920, working in the experimental and racing department. 'Hassan' Bentleys today

are still a highlight among members of the Bentley Drivers'
Club. As did 'Lofty' England, Walter Hassan joined the E.R.A.
team, then at Bourne, and became Superintendent of the
E.R.A. Racing Car assembly unit. This was followed by a
year at Brooklands with Thomson and Taylor, until in 1938
Lyons persuaded him to join him as development engineer.
For a three-year period during the war he was seconded to
Bristol Aero Engines, but returned to Jaguar for seven years in
1943, again as development engineer.

Why did Lyons need such an extensive team around him?
For one thing, he realized that the overnight success of the
S.S. was only the beginning. It was, as Henly's said, 'Long,
low, and very fast.' But there was still much of the Standard
parentage, and Lyons knew that by careful streamlining of
Coventry industry he could produce a car which would be
completely to his specification, and which would owe little if
anything to the old L-head Standard Sixteen engine.

The interim stage was the hotting-up of the S.S.1 to give
it far better sporting performance. Under Heynes' direction
the axle ratio was changed from 4·66 to 4·25 : 1, and engine
modifications were made using a high-lift camshaft with altered
overlap. The maximum performance was an honest 90 m.p.h.,
so naturally the car was dubbed the S.S.90. And roughly ninety
of these cars were built before there came a major change and
eventually the S.S.100 was introduced.

This change was an o.h.v. engine which Heynes and
others had spent months in developing. The prototype was a
2,663·7 c.c. six-cylinder push-rod engine developing 102 b.h.p.
Later a bored-out 3½-litre version was produced developing
about 120 b.h.p. Although new in many respects, the team had
been instructed to use standard components if possible, so that
Lyons need not be compelled to tool up for production if
greater economy could be effected by leaving assembly to
Standards.

This engine was a success from the outset, and during 1936
it was decided to install it in the open sports S.S.90. Two versions were produced, the 2½-litre and the 3½-litre, and the
model was immediately dubbed the S.S.100. There had never
been a sports car quite like it, and its nearest competitor
was the Meadows-engined 4½-litre Lagonda MG45 and LG45,

which were listed at £1,000. The S.S.100 was priced at £445 for the open two-seater.

Although the S.S.100 was regarded as a rather 'fancy' sports car by the older racing fraternity, it did clock up an impressive list of victories in the Marne Grand Prix, International Alpine Trial, Monte Carlo Rally and other events. And in reply to critics who said that the '100' was merely salesmanship, *The Autocar* road-test of the 3½-litre S.S.100, published in September 1938, gave the best timed speed over the quarter-mile as 101·12 m.p.h., and mean maximum timed speed over the quarter-mile as 98·1 m.p.h. Acceleration figures were impressive, too, for a car weighing only a shade under 24 cwt. (0·77 lb. per c.c.), as it took only 3·8 seconds to reach 30 m.p.h. from stand-still, through the gears, and 10·4 seconds to attain 60 m.p.h. Fuel consumption was found to be in the 16–18 m.p.g. range, and a brake test in dry weather gave a stopping distance of 27·5 feet from 30 m.p.h. on concrete.

Five years after that test was made, the world was at war, and motoring nostalgia was kept alive by magazine series such as 'Talking of Sports Cars', in which the Sports Editor recalled:

> 'I think that these 100's would surprise a lot of drivers by the punch they possess. . . . If a satisfactory formula could be evolved to evaluate and compare acceleration or maximum speed in terms of £ cost in original price, I think it would be found that the 100—more particularly the 3½—would come out among the first three cars on the market. . . .'

Why, then, did not Lyons decide to build the new and so successful engine in his own factory? Simply that he was far-sighted, and had set his eyes on an even wider horizon. Captain Black's machine shops were well equipped to produce the new 2,663-c.c. engine, and to take it over would have hampered development at Foleshill at a time when Lyons was secretly planning to produce not a new engine, but a complete new car. It is now no secret that this caused disappointment among some members of the design team, who had hoped that after getting 120 b.h.p. and 100 genuine miles an hour from the new unit, Sir William would have appointed his own produc-

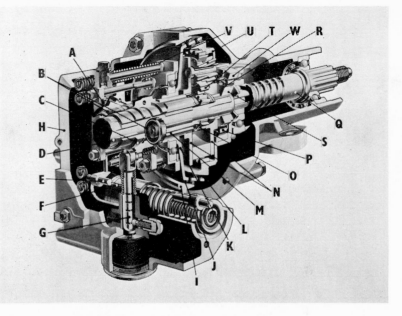

Cut-away diagram showing internal construction of the Laycock de Norman-ville positive overdrive. This overdrive comprises an epicyclic gear-train in which planet wheels revolve round the sun wheel and inside the annulus. Its ingenuity is in the hydraulic operation, whereby the transmission of power passes through the overdrive whether it is in operation or not

Layout of the Arnott supercharger, fitted to Jaguar 2·4

Victorious trio—Sir William Lyons (*centre*), David Murray (Le Patron of the Ecurie Ecosse) and (*right*) W. E. 'Wilkie' Wilkinson. Sir William was asked by Rossleigh, the Edinburgh distributors, to present a silver cigarette box to the Ecurie Ecosse team. The team receives all its supplies through distributors, and not direct from the Jaguar factory

tion team to build it. When they were shown his plans for chassis and coachwork, however, they were forced to admit that it was much better tactics to concentrate the still-limited resources of their Coventry plant on the task they knew best, leaving engine assembly to Standards.

Nobody disputed the craftsmanship which Black's team put into this special Lyons' project, and as for design, the *Automotive Engineer*, reviewing the new o.h.v. unit, commented that:

'The crankcase and crankshaft have been strengthened to deal with the increased power output, the connecting-rods being of RR–56 alloy with white-metal bearings. The cylinder block is of chromidium iron, and Nelson Bohnalite pistons without split skirt are employed. The overhead valves are in line, the inlet valve being larger than the exhaust. The inlet ports are fed from a gallery that runs the full length of the head, and is machined straight through.'

Meanwhile, long before the S.S.100 began to establish itself at Marne and at Brooklands, Lyons was ready for his major move. The new car had first to be given a name.

'One day when the model was almost ready,' said Wayne Mineau on one occasion in the *Daily Mail*, 'Lyons rang his advertising department. "Bring me a list of names," he said, "of insects, animals, birds and fish." On to his desk went a typewritten array of 500 creatures that walked, crawled, swam or flew. Within the hour Lyons made his brilliant choice. 'I like the sound of Jaguar,' he said. 'It has everything we want—power, speed and grace.'

Sir William Lyons and Bill Rankin have since strenuously denied this, and assert that it did not happen that way. But it is still an amusing story, even if apocryphal. A very real difficulty was that many suitable 'animal' names were already in use for cars or aircraft—notably Eagle, Lynx, Hawk, Tiger, Viper, Hornet, Gamecock and Greyhound. Moreover in producing a car for international sale it is imperative to use a trade-name which can reasonably be pronounced in most normal languages—as those who market everything from Esso to Oxo are well aware. In this respect Jaguar filled the bill, except that Britons usually call it 'Jag-you-ah', while Americans know it as 'Jag-war'.

Bill Rankin's Press and trade presentation of the sensational new model at London's Mayfair Hotel will be long-remembered. The Airline version of the S.S.1 had already endeared itself to enthusiastic drivers, and this model—again partly inspired by suggestions made by Geoffrey Smith, managing editor of *The Autocar*—was current in 1934-5. Press and public alike were no doubt expecting something similar, but lower, even sleeker, with even more luxurious armchair-leather chairs. . . .

The new S.S. Jaguar was concealed behind curtains at the Mayfair Hotel, and when these were drawn apart the 200 hard-bitten trade and Press guests burst into spontaneous applause at what they saw. And what they saw was a smart, black four-door saloon which certainly owed a little to the Park Ward 3½-litre Bentley, but with rather smaller proportions and neater lines. At the front was a new, clean-cut deep radiator with stoneguard, and a large, flat filler-cap. The body was of steel on ash framing, with upholstery in Vaumol hide. The 2½-litre engine was rated at 19·5 h.p., and other chassis features included Burman-Douglas worm-and-nut steering and Girling brakes.

The audience, after the initial burst of applause, sat puzzled. Here was a £1,000 motor-car, of a different price-class from any in which William Lyons had previously succeeded. Noting their hesitation, he asked for slips of paper to be passed around, and critics were invited to write down their estimate of the list price. The average guess ran to £750; the lowest possible estimate being £450. Then, when the tension was at its greatest, Lyons himself stood up and said: 'Well, gentlemen. None of you has the correct figure. The price of the new S.S. Jaguar is—£385!'

This car, the first Jaguar, was seen publicly at the 1935 Olympia show, where the public confirmed the opinion of the trade experts.

The Hon. Brian Lewis was already clocking up records for the old S.S.90 in such events as the R.A.C. Rally. The S.S.100, powered by a similar engine to that of the S.S. Jaguar, went on to achieve success at Marne, in the R.A.C. Rally, and at Brooklands. Other models of the S.S. Jaguar were produced, including the four-cylinder 1½-litre model which was in direct competition with M.G.

At this point Lyons, realizing how far his organization had developed since the days of the Swallow Side Car Company, making pretty bodies for Austin Sevens, decided to turn S.S. Cars Limited into a public company. There were a number of internal changes, resulting from Bill Walmsley's wish to resign and leave Lyons to develop his own policy, and the next year was one of consolidation of past progress, made easier with the working capital obtained through the company transaction.

By 1939 Jaguar styling was influenced by Bugatti, and one prototype Jaguar fixed-head coupé was built which bears a certain resemblance to the Gangloff-bodied Type 57 designed by Jean Bugatti—with the exception that Heynes, Hassan and the rest of the team, although fascinated by the straight-eight, were concentrating on interesting studies concerned with push-rod and o.h.c. four- and six-cylinder units.

These studies, in common with many others, were interrupted by war, when under the shadow-factory plan the Coventry works was switched to aircraft production.

Today Jaguar own their ultra-modern factory on Browns Lane, to the north of Coventry, just off the A-45. You are greeted in the luxurious entrance hall by a life-size bronze jaguar, and the other end of the hall is graced with a beautiful copy of the Annigoni portrait of Her Majesty the Queen. This factory gives employment to over 4,000 on a full five-day week, and vast batteries of Maximatics, Landis, Churchills, Newells and Hey lappers produce a flow of some seventy cars every twenty-four hours. The Hey lappers, installed during the war when Jaguars were making tank engines, are among the few relics of the days when this was a Daimler-group shadow factory.

All this commercial success, as well as an important facet of national prosperity and pride, is due in recent years to one line of automobile development known by two initials—not 'S.S.' (which was finally dropped when the company title was changed to Jaguar Cars Limited), but 'XK'.

How the XK engine design came into being is one of the greatest British engineering stories of achievement.

Three

THE XK ENGINE

'THE Jaguar car has proved itself in no uncertain manner, and Sir William Lyons, Mr. Heynes and all concerned are to be congratulated on a most remarkable feat in producing an automobile of such high efficiency at a popular price. . . .'

The speaker was one of the most distinguished automobile designers of all time, Mr. Georges Roesch, M.I.MECH.E., designer of the Talbot which was so effectively demonstrated in the 1930 Le Mans 24-hour race. Praise from Roesch (who today is a gas-turbine expert, and one of Britain's leading metallurgists) is high praise indeed, and the occasion was the meeting of the Automobile Division of The Institution of Mechanical Engineers, when for the first time Jaguar Cars allowed a detailed analysis of the XK engine to be made before experts.

Sir William Lyons himself gave a postscript to the story of the XK development when, as S.M.M. & T. president, he had asked: 'I wonder how many of the public appreciate that the new model which a manufacturer presents for their approval may often owe the form it takes, and the qualities it possesses, to the scrapping of a dozen or more prototypes in the course of two or three years. . . .'

This does not mean Heynes and his team—a team then comprising C. W. Baily and Walter Hassan—were faced with a whole succession of 'things that went wrong'. But the Jaguar company now makes no secret of the various research policy lines, and in retrospect it is interesting to see what went on in the months immediately following the end of the 1939–45 war, at a time when the company was marketing the Mk. IV as a stop-gap. This was in all major respects similar to the pre-war model, as was the case with most other British manufacturers. With Jaguar, however, the model was better received as the design was well advanced, even in November 1945 when the

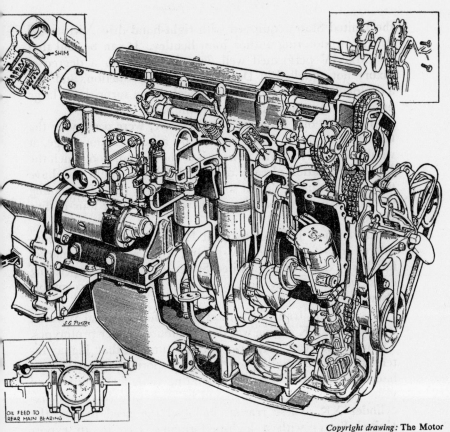

SHIM →

OIL FEED TO
REAR MAIN BEARING

Cut-away drawing of the XK engine, which is basically the same for all variants from the XK120 to the XK150 and XK-SS. The small inset diagrams give details of valve cap and shim for clearance adjustment, the method of removing timing chain, and the main bearing oil feeds

first post-war 3½-litre saloons began rolling off the ex-aircraft assembly lines. The same 25·01-h.p. engine was used, such a satisfactory unit that no one outside the Jaguar research team had an inkling that behind the scenes something revolutionary was planned.

The target was not only the U.S. market, although American motorists might be forgiven for imagining it was so.

'The Mark IV was produced so swiftly that it came over to

the United States equipped with right-hand drive,' wrote the American motoring author John Bentley. 'It can be said that the Mk. IV performed well, was finished with a degree of luxury not equalled in Detroit post-war production, and had a decidedly "classic" look that appealed to a surprisingly large number of American motoring enthusiasts. . . .'

Problems of a different sort, however, were occupying the Coventry team. If there were to be a new engine range, it would obviously be wise to keep it to those groups on which the Jaguar reputation already depended. And it would also have to be an advanced design so that the whole cost of re-tooling would not need to be met again within another four or five years.

It can now be disclosed that Heynes' team seriously considered a V-8, and also a V-12, but while a potential market for these existed in the United States, taxation and operating costs would possibly not make such units very acceptable elsewhere.

As actually transpired, most of the fundamental research work for the XK engine was done on four-cylinder prototypes. Through the years there were trade rumours that Jaguar intended to list a smaller, four-cylinder sports car, but Heynes had very sound reasons for suggesting that, for a number of years at least, production should be concentrated on the six-cylinder XK. These reasons included the need to face the United States with a high-performance car, in an export market where only a small minority care for the qualities inherent in a typical British small sports car. A large engine, running well within its limits, yet capable of propelling a saloon at a genuine 100 m.p.h., was the target set. One important factor made this target easier to achieve; the factory was to be specially tooled-up for production, so the designers did not have to bother themselves overmuch about existing tooling.

First let us see the specification of the XK engine as finally evolved, and used in the first XK-120.

The six-cylinder 3½-litre engine has twin overhead camshafts at an angle of 70 degrees, driven by a two-stage duplex roller chain. Actual capacity is 3,442 c.c. (83 mm. bore and 106 mm. stroke). It develops 160 b.h.p. at 5,000 r.p.m. The unit has large non-adjustable and directly operated valves, and

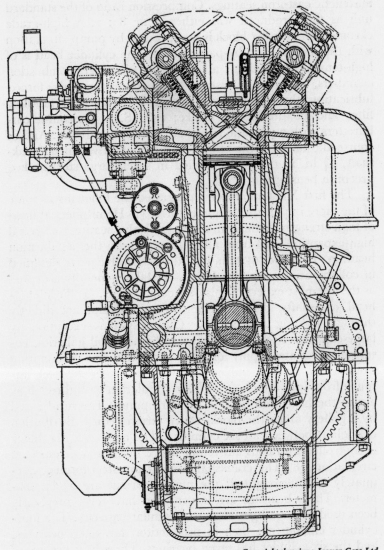

Cross-sectional diagram of the **XK** engine, showing porting,
valve gear-drive layout and major block and crankcase
construction

austenetic cast-iron seatings. Compression ratio of the standard unit as first produced was either 7 or 8 : 1. A high-grade chrome iron cylinder block is used, cooled by pump circulation with thermostat- and by-pass-control. The cylinder head is of high-tensile aluminium alloy, with spherical combustion chambers, aluminium pistons, steel connecting-rods, forced lubrication throughout by submerged pump with full-flow filter and floating gauze intake; twin S.U. horizontal car-buretters with automatic choke electrically controlled. And of course the heart of the engine is the counterweighted crank-shaft, $2\frac{3}{4}$ in. in diameter, carried in seven large steel-backed precision bearings.

The first XK announcement stressed the following as some of the more important design features: (1) Hemispherical head of high-strength aluminium alloy. (2) Valve seatings of special high-expansion cast-iron alloy shrunk into the combustion head. (3) Induction system, including the valve ports, designed in collaboration with Mr. Harry Weslake, generally accepted as the foremost expert in this particular aspect. (4) Twin over-head camshafts, driven by a two-stage chain, act directly through floating tappets. (5) Oiling system—exceptionally large-capacity oil-pump with large-diameter oil galleries, en-suring adequate supply of cool lubricant, and eliminating frothing. (6) Exhaust valves of high-grade austenetic steel, im-mune from lead attack. (7) Water circulation with direct flow across the head from a high-pressure pump. The head is fed by a gallery along the block, which ensures equal distribution of coolant between all six cylinders. The cooling to the block is controlled at a constant temperature by means of restricted circulation. (8) The crankshaft is a 65-ton steel forging, ade-quately counterweighted; the main bearings are $2\frac{3}{4}$ in. dia-meter. These bearings are larger than have ever previously been used on passenger engines of similar capacity. The four-cylinder engine (not then in production) has three bearings, and the six-cylinder has seven bearings. These bearings are of the Vandervell thin-shell type, and have shown on test to have practically unlimited life. (9) Pistons are of Aerolite aluminium alloy, fitted with chromium-plated top rings, which tests show give over 100 per cent increase in life to the bores.

This, then, was the maker's own technical analysis in brief

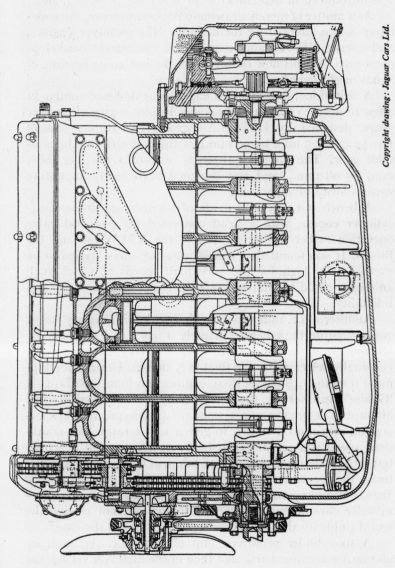

Longitudinal cross-sectional drawing of the **XK** engine

of the XK engine, at a time when the first XK-120 sports tourer was introduced in September 1948 at a basic price of £988.

As a matter of merely drawing-office convenience, the code-letter X was adopted for the designs of the prototype engines, and a series XF, XG and so on was run in extensive development tests. All this now comes under the intriguing heading of 'what might have been'.

A twin o.h.c. four-cylinder engine was designed similar in a few respects to the classic Lagonda Rapier engine of pre-war years, designed by I. Tim Aschcroft. The Rapier was of 1,104 c.c. (62·5 mm. by 90 mm.), with chain-driven o.h. camshaft gear. The Jaguar prototype was of 1,360 c.c. (66·5 mm. by 98 mm.), and was designed particularly for testing various forms of valve gear.

A bench test was then made of a somewhat similar four-cylinder engine, with a head converted for push-rod valve operation rather similar to that of the B.M.W.328 and the Bristol. It was found that valve-spring pressures needed to be exceptionally high for the very high speeds at which such an engine could be run, and this mitigated against silence and reliability.

Another o.h.c. unit was then designed, with slightly larger swept volume than before, namely 1,996 c.c. (80·5 mm. by 98 mm.), and here the valve gear was very similar to that eventually selected for the final XK design. During development tests in 1948 one of these engines was loaned to Lt.-Col. 'Goldie' Gardner for the 2-litre class World Speed Record attempt. The engine was a standard prototype, with the exception of pistons modified to give a 12 : 1 ratio. Safe crankshaft speed was estimated to be 6,500 r.p.m., and a bench-test showed that it developed 146 b.h.p. at 6,000 r.p.m. 'Goldie' broke the record in the 2-litre class at 176 m.p.h., but as the Jaguar company was not then intending to produce a four-cylinder car the success of this attempt did not receive the world publicity that otherwise might have been the case.

A six-cylinder prototype unit of 3,200 c.c. (83 mm. by 98 mm.) was constructed, and then in the final XK version the stroke was increased to 106 mm., so giving a swept volume of 3,448 c.c. The main reason for this change was the need for additional power at low crankshaft speeds.

This XK engine was installed in the now-familiar 120-type chassis of 8 ft. 6 in. wheelbase, front track 4 ft. 3 in. and rear 4 ft. 2 in. The frame was a straight plane steel box section of great strength, and torsional rigidity was ensured by large box-section cross-members. Independent front suspension was used incorporating transverse wishbones and long torsion bars with Newton telescopic-type hydraulic shock-absorbers. The rear suspension was by long silico-manganese steel half-elliptic springs controlled by Girling PV7 hydraulic shockers. Brakes at the outset were Lockheed full hydraulic, 12-in. drums, two leading-shoe front, giving a total friction lining area of 207 square inches.

Transmission was by four-speed single helical synchromesh box, with ground-teeth gears running on needle bearings, with synchromesh on all but bottom and reverse. Standard ratios were 12·29 1st, 7·22 2nd, 4·98 3rd and 3·64 top, while optional ratios of 3·27, 4·0 and 4·3 were available. Transmission included Borg & Beck 10-in. diameter single dry plate clutch, and Hardy-Spicer propeller shaft with needle-roller bearings.

The car was received at the Earls Court exhibition with great praise from technicians, trade and public. Mr. Boddy, editor of *Motor Sport*, said:

'By the high quality of its finish and appointments alone the XK120 represents very good value for money. Its very liberal speed and acceleration, accomplished with such willing ease, are unrivalled, and to drive this Jaguar is to enjoy an experience at once unique, and embracing one of the highest pinnacles of modern motoring.'

In a detailed road test of the XK120 the same journal reported:

'I saw 120 m.p.h. recorded along a mile or so of straight road, and colleagues using the Southend Arterial "clocked" 130. This represents a true 120 m.p.h., and I would put the genuine two-way maximum at approximately 110 m.p.h. The surge of acceleration from 80 m.p.h. onwards is, per-haps, more exhilarating than these impressive maximum speeds. . . . For a car good for 100 m.p.h. almost anywhere the XK120 is notably docile in conception and demeanour. It runs very cool, the water temperature mostly below 60°C. . . . The facia is devoid of masses of switches and dials; it even incorporates a cigar-lighter (fancy smoking a *cigar* in an XK!). . . .'

Subsequent tests by this and other journals showed that, as was naturally to be expected, the 120 had certain minor teething troubles, and racing emphasized these. Overheating was a difficulty at first, and the Lockheed twin-leading-shoe front brakes were apt to give symptoms of fade after application at speed. These matters were dealt with.

It can now be disclosed that both the six-cylinder and four-cylinder versions of the XK were fitted by the factory into disguised cars, and driven hard over the Continent, so most of the minor teething troubles were soon discovered. The camouflaged coachwork was not so low as that of the final XK sports tourer, and this may be one reason why the radiator overheating was at first not detected as a potential defect.

In France a motoring columnist saw one of the prototype XK's and became convinced that, although the vehicle bore British registration, it was a 'plant' by Alfa-Romeo or Ferrari to conceal their new racing design, and he plagued the life out of hotel and garage staff who might know anything about the new hush-hush car.

It was an amusing parallel with that occasion in the nineteen-twenties when W. O. Bentley took the prototype of the 6½-litre across to Le Mans. The car was fitted with a stately four-door six-light limousine and a dummy radiator shell similar to a Sizaire-Berwick to hide the true identity from prying eyes, and for the entire duration of the race the car was parked right up to a hoarding, with a tarpaulin roped round the bonnet.

The prototype Jags needed no such screening, as the Continental tour was carried out at great speed. Moreover, while all these secret tests were being carried out in the Alps, and on the *autobahnen* and *routes nationales*, the company had decided to issue the Mk. V as a stop-gap. This had the 2½-litre and 3½-litre engines as alternatives; coachwork design was modernized from the Mk. IV, but performance was stepped up by increasing compression ratio to 6·75 to 1, so giving 125 b.h.p. at 4,250 r.p.m. This car, marketed in January 1949 at £1,263 (including tax), left a large section of the trade convinced that all these stories of a completely new Jaguar were so much hot air, and it was generally believed that Lyons in common with other magnates was still pinning his faith to push-rod-operated valves, and a lusty engine peaking at less than 5,000 r.p.m.

It was only natural that when the XK120 made its sensational appearance it received the 'knock' from a few rival sections of the industry who were quick to give the impression that it was too good to be true, that Lyons would never be able to get the car into actual series production at this price. There was, as a matter of fact, a short gap before cars came off the line fast enough to justify full-scale production, and this gave another opportunity for rumour. Critics and production engineers of some rival groups were saying that it would be an almost impossible task to produce an engine of this type at a rate of more than a dozen or so a week.

Internal details of the XK engine were criticized, too. They said the head was too light, at 50 lb., and that in cast iron (at about 110 lb.) it would obviously be too heavy; on the other hand such a complex head could not be mass-produced without risk of damage. Why, machine-shop operatives would only have to bruise a batch of heads by knocking or dropping them, and this would surely hold up an entire week's production.

Others, still criticizing on the score that it was too cheap to be true, said Heynes should have the head cast in a high silicon alloy, with cast-iron inserts for seating and valve guides. It was doubted if such an engine could be adequately balanced on assembly, and critics visualized lengthy bench-tests and stripping down of faulty engines. The steel rods were criticized. The complex double chain-drive for camshafts was criticized, and Heynes was asked why he did not use a single chain, as is done by Ferrari and some other Continentals. . . .

All these criticisms (the technical answers to which we shall see later in this chapter) added up to one mounting cynicism: *It can't be as good as it's cracked up to be.* In the spring of 1949 Lyons and Heynes hit on a plan, amplified by Bill Rankin, to kill this sort of rumour for good and all.

They decided to take a perfectly standard XK, carrying full equipment even to front bumper, GB plate and touring accessories, drive it to Belgium and give it a full-throttle run on the Jabbeke–Aeltre motor road, and see what the car could do when timed officially by the R.A.C. de Belgique.

A team of Jaguar executives went out with the car, accompanied by well-known representatives of other firms and organizations, including Colonel Barnes of the R.A.C., and a Dunlop representative who was to supervise the Road Speed 16 × 6·00 tyres used on the run.

At Rankin's suggestion the run—which, to be frank, was highly tentative for a sports car as then untried in public—was to be made a focal point of European motor correspondents. A big group of British journalists was flown to Ostend and taken to the Jabbeke highway by Belgian Iso Bloc coaches, while similar transport was provided for many foreign correspondents. The whole gay affair began to take on the air of a miniature Le Mans.

As it happened, the focal point at first was not the cream, left-hand drive XK120, but the driver. Chosen for this historic series of runs was the late R. M. V. Sutton, aged fifty-three at the time of the test, whose exploits many years previously with Alvis and Lea-Francis will be well remembered. In his time he had been a Rolls-Royce draughtsman, a leading technical man at Daimlers, and he made a great name in the early days of Brooklands, racing Lea-Francis with Kaye Don, and Brooklands Riley Nines with Joan Richmond, Elsie Wisdom and Major C. M. Harvey. Eventually he joined the Jaguar Development Division, and was rightly chosen for the Jabbeke run. It was Sutton, too, who drove the racy-looking, 1½-litre, four-cylinder prototype XK, with its air-strut suspension, on which so much of the development work for the final six-cylinder car was done.

'When the XK120 was designed,' Sutton recorded afterwards, 'it was obvious that the "120" indicated the car's maximum speed, but it was very necessary first to find out if it could do this. That was the factory's instruction. I was equally concerned to find out if *I* could do this! Well, naturally I had a few secret misgivings, which I kept strictly to myself, about my own capabilities. After all my fastest-ever had been 110 m.p.h. at Brooklands on a Lea-Francis 21 years previously.

In order to put this to the test, I set out alone in the very early hours of the morning to a five-mile straight I know near Coventry, and which would be deserted at that hour. The car was handling well, and I made the first run quite well. It seemed very fast indeed—but I was too busy driving to watch clocks. Then subsequent runs, although carried out at the same speed, seemed to me to be slower, and I had time to read the instruments carefully now. The rev.-counter was touching 5,200 r.p.m., equivalent to a road-speed of slightly over 130 m.p.h.!

I returned to the works feeling very pleased with myself, but although everyone was polite they were rather sceptical. However, later tests confirmed my findings, and the "120" was officially adopted.'

His results at Jabbeke were certainly astounding. Using ordinary Shell pump fuel, the car exceeded a speed of 130 m.p.h. On 30th May 1949, when officially timed by the Royal Automobile Club of Belgium, a maximum speed of 132·6 m.p.h. over the flying mile was easily attained on the Jabbeke–Aeltre road. A speed of 126·448 m.p.h. was attained on the f.s. two-way mile with hood and screen erect. A normal scuttle deflector was then substituted for the screen and a faired undershield fitted (this was a standard extra on the original XK120), and the speed rose to 132·36 m.p.h. for the f.s. two-way kilometre, and the best run was one kilometre at 133·388 m.p.h. A series of standing-start runs was then attempted, where Sutton's skill in handling the car counted for much. The standing-kilometre run was done at 74·168 m.p.h., and the standing mile at 86·43 m.p.h. No tyre troubles nor any mechanical trouble worth recording were experienced, despite the fact that the car must have travelled a total of some fifty miles at high speeds all of over 120 m.p.h.

Still in his blue overalls, sporting his B.R.D.C. badge, Sutton drove quietly on to the gala reception by the Deputy Mayor of Ostend, and the truly international party drank the health of the '120', of Sir William Lyons, of Sutton. . . . And back home in Britain there was not so much talk about the car that looked 'too good to be true'.

Sutton subsequently left Jaguar to become chief tester for Alvis, and as a proud postscript to the Jabbeke story it can be recorded that in October 1953—four years later—Jaguar sent Norman Dewis (then chief driver for the company) back to Jabbeke–Aeltre with a specially prepared XK120 in which he broke the world's stock-production car record for the flying mile, with a phenomenal new time of 172·412 m.p.h.

Within a year of its introduction to the sporting public, the XK120 was winning international laurels. The Jabbeke record of course was a works matter, but the following records and successes were achieved by private owners.

In the One Hour International Production Car Race at Silverstone, 1949, Jaguars were placed first and second, winning the race outright and returning the fastest lap speed of the race. This was the August B.R.D.C.—*Daily Express* Trophy meeting, in which demonstration runs were made by such giants as John Cobb and 'Goldie' Gardner.

The Production Car Race was the event of the day, however, for after the Jabbeke record everyone was anxious to know what sort of showing would be made by the Jaguars of Bira, Leslie Johnson and Peter Walker, in a race which featured also such experienced drivers as Rolt, Allard, Louis Chiron and Wisdom.

At the height of excitement of the event, Bira's blue Jag spun when a tyre burst, at the very moment Leslie Johnson was right on his tail. Extremely clever driving by them both averted disaster, but the unfortunate burst—due, it was found, to accidental fitting of a touring-type tube in a racing cover—prevented a 1–2–3 Jaguar placing. Had it been so, the cars would have passed the line in red, white and blue order, which was surely something on which even Bill Rankin could not improve, publicity-wise. Although a tyre fault prevented this, the One-Hour Production Car Race was nevertheless a victory for Jaguar, Leslie Johnson completing 28 laps at an average of 82·8 m.p.h., and Peter Walker averaged the same distance at 82·29 m.p.h., coming home just five seconds later, and with one lap at 84·9 m.p.h. to his credit.

'*Jaguar Continues to Make Motoring History*,' announced

Rankin in his advertising, and it was certainly a fine beginning with so much more to follow.

At the race meeting promoted in January 1950 by the A.A.A., the Production Car Race was won by a Jaguar which also gained the special award for the best performance of a British car. This was the first chief impact of the new XK120 on the sporting section of the American public, and in Europe, too, the new model achieved gratifying success in the International Alpine Trial of 1950. This, the most severe of European trials, extends over five days and covers the worst mountain roads and passes of Switzerland and France for some 2,000 miles. In the face of determined opposition from a hundred competitors driving some thirty makes of car, a Jaguar returned the best performance of any car, irrespective of class or size, and won the Alpine Cup. It was also placed first in its class, returned fastest time in the flying kilometre, fastest time in acceleration and braking test, fastest time in timed climbs, and won eight other awards!

The Production Car Race at Silverstone, which had been such an opening victory for Jaguar in 1949, was again a scene of great success in 1950. This time Jaguar finished 1st, 2nd, 4th and 5th in the Unlimited class, and also won the team prize. The '120' went on to sweep the board in the 1950 T.T. Not only did a Jaguar win the race and the Trophy outright, but Jaguars were placed 1st, 2nd and 3rd in their class, and won the team prize and the award for the greatest distance covered.

Stirling Moss in his *Book of Motor Sport* (Cassell) wrote after the first successful Production Car Race at Silverstone:

'For myself, I was a trifle gloomy, for in the programme was an entirely new race for standard sports cars—in which I had no part. Jaguar XK120's were appearing for the first time. I made no bones about my longing to race one, but it seemed that no one was much interested in a nineteen-year-old lacking any experience of sports-car racing. . . .'

However, Stirling did win the T.T. for Jaguar at record speed in the rain, and as a leading U.S. commentator admitted: 'It was an omen for Moss, who developed into one of the

world's greatest racing drivers, and the Jag, which was already
one of the world's best racing cars. They teamed up many
times after that memorable date, and have brought back to
England *more prizes and awards than any other racing car* in British
automobile history.'

There were still two more major victories for the XK engine
in 1950, however, to confound critics. An indication of the
engine's power and stamina was given when the following
world water-speed records were set up on Lake Windermere by
an 800-kg. craft fitted with a standard XK power-unit: 1-hour
record at 55·58 statute m.p.h., previously held by Germany;
24-hour nautical miles record at 63·53 m.p.h., previously held
by Germany, and the 3-hour record at 51·62 statute m.p.h.
previously held by Italy.

To cap it all, on 24th to 25th October 1950 an XK120 was
driven in three-hour spells by two drivers during a 24-hour
period at an average speed of 107·46 m.p.h. In the final hour,
after 23 hours' faultless running, an average of 112·4 m.p.h.
was returned, with one lap at 121·4 m.p.h. This performance
was officially observed by the A.C. de France, at the Montlhery
track, and it so captured the imagination of all sporting motorists that, two years later, Lyons decided to sponsor an even
harder marathon.

In August 1952 he sent a production car again to Montlhery, this time with Leslie Johnson heading a team comprising
Stirling Moss, J. E. G. Fairman and H. L. Hadley. Their instructions were blunt and brief. 'Drive the car,' said the Works
instructions, 'all out, stopping only for fuel and to change tyres
and drivers.'

The test began in the afternoon of 5th August, and continued for the scheduled non-stop week. At the end of the
gruelling run it was found that the car had been driven non-
stop for 168 hours at an average speed of 100·31 m.p.h. A distance of 16,851·73 miles was covered in the seven days and
nights, equal to about two years' normal driving.

This would have constituted a world record, so it was of less
importance that on this run the car had also broken the following records: 72 hours at 105·55 m.p.h. (world and class records); 10,000 kilometres at 107·31 m.p.h. (class record);
96 hours at 101·17 m.p.h. (world and class records); 15,000

kilometres at 101·95 m.p.h. (world and class); 10,000 miles at 100·65 m.p.h. (world and class).

Although no doubt elated at this success, Lyons was anxious to show the stamina of the car, so he instructed a report to be prepared by the Shell laboratory, and this read as follows:

'The general condition of the engine was excellent, and had the engine not been dismantled there was no apparent reason why it should not have given satisfactory service for many thousands of miles of normal hard driving. Crankshaft wear was so low that, in spite of the car having covered nearly 17,000 miles on the record run, plus just under 2,000 miles previously, the crankshaft was still within production tolerances, and would have been passed by the inspection department for installation in a new car.

Bore wear was not abnormal, showing a maximum of 3–3·5 thousandths at the top of the bore, after a total mileage of about 18,708. All the pistons were in good condition apart from slight erosions on the top of one, while rings were bedded perfectly in the bore, and the absence of carbon deposits was particularly noticeable. The sump was free from sludge, as were also the camshaft covers. The cylinder head was virtually free from deposit, and the seats, both inlet and exhaust, were in a very satisfactory condition.

All valves were seating perfectly, although slight pitting and blackening of the surface of the exhaust valves had occurred. The standard-type plugs, which had run the total distance, were in astonishingly good condition. . . . The rear axle cover-plate was removed and the crown wheel and differential examined. The axle was in perfect condition as far as could be seen, both faces of the crown wheel having an excellent finish, and the differential gears still showing some of the original machining marks.'

All this, after 16,851 miles non-stop, for seven days and nights, 168 hours at an average of over 100 m.p.h. This was surely the effective reply to critics of the XK engine, and of its design and production.

The production manager of Jaguar Cars Ltd., John Silver, was able to give the lie to the story that the engine was so complex it could be produced only in small quantities per week. In truth, even by the end of 1950, the production was approximately 250 engines a month. Each engine is run-in for four hours on the bench, using coal-gas, a single gas carburetter feeding the twin S.U.s. A further three-hour run is then given at about 2,500 r.p.m., stepped up by further one-hour runs to a maximum of 3,000 r.p.m. During this final run a flash full-throttle test is given, a tolerance of plus-or-minus 5 b.h.p. being observed. The engine, fitted to the chassis, is then road-tested. That was the initial test schedule of the 120, and today similar but improved and prolonged tests are made.

Jaguar users in the United States and other countries have available variants such as the XK120 M, XK120 MC and so on. It must be stressed that basically these cars and power units are identical, and indeed the master servicing manual for the XK120 applies in nearly every particular to all these variants. Jaguar owners in countries outside Great Britain need have no fear that their 'hot' version is mechanically very different from the stock job.

Detailed specifications of all the stock versions of Jaguar are given at the end of this book, but it should be noted that the differences between, say, the stock 120, the M and the MC are differences of output performance rather than of mechanics.

For example, the compression ratio of the stock XK120, 120 M, MC, stock XK140 and 140 MC is in each case 8 to 1, and the total displacement remains (American rating) at 210 cu. in. Compression ratio of the XK-SS is 9 to 1, as in the D-type. In a later section details of the different types of rear axle are given, but it should be noted here that the axle ratio of the stock XK120 is 3·54 to 1, and this applies to *all* models such as the 120 MC, the XK140, XK140 MC and of course the XK150, with but two exceptions. These exceptions are the XK120 M, which is generally available in the United States with a 3·77 ratio rear axle, and the XK-SS which was distributed as stock with a 3·77 axle.

The first critics of the XK engine had made certain points and now, after the convincing road and track victories, Heynes was able to explain how the various technical details were met.

The chain drive for camshafts was criticized, and it was explained that in one of the prototype XK engines a single

An historic Jaguar group, after the Le Mans win in 1953. Seen here at the pits are (*left to right*) Len Haydn (Chief Mechanic), J. Duncan Hamilton and Tony Rolt (the winning team), William Heynes (designer of the car), Mrs. Rolt, Mrs. Duncan Hamilton, Sir William Lyons, Miss Weston and (*extreme right*) Lady Lyons

When every second counts. Pit stop in the 1957 Le Mans. Ivor Bueb leaps from the Jaguar cockpit as mechanics take their appointed places for refuelling and tyre changes

W. E. 'Wilkie' Wilkinson checking the plugs on the eve of the 1957 Monza. The cars had been driven fast from Le Mans to Monza, with a detour to the Riviera because of flooded Alpine passes, and there was a tremendous amount of work to be done at the last moment prior to Monza. On the car shown, the same plugs were used as at Le Mans

chain with one adjustable sprocket, plus sprocket drive for oil-pump and distributor, had been tested, and although it operated successfully, the peculiar thrashing, high-pitched whine could not be checked. Rubber-mounted jockey sprockets and other devices were tried, but it was not found possible to devise this method of driving the camshafts with a degree of silence acceptable to sporting motorists who expect reasonable quiet in a closed car. Many months were spent in these chain tests, and in fact the present drive system is modified from that on the prototype, the camshaft sprockets now being adjustable to a fine degree.

The method of valve operation had been criticized by opponents of the o.h.c. system, and it was stressed that Roesch in his Le Mans Talbots had so reduced reciprocating weight by use of light push-rods and special rocker design that the total reciprocating weight was reduced to 8·8 oz. per valve. The fitted valve load in the Talbot was also 90 lb. against the XK engine's 102 lb. It was also true that an engine with Roesch valve gear, fitted in W. M. Couper's Alpine Trial car, lapped Brooklands in 1938 at an officially timed speed of 129·7 m.p.h. While this is so, Heynes was able to show that the usual push-rod system has a total average weight of 18·4 oz., and that the XK engine design involves a total weight per valve (i.e. valve, spring, cap, etc.) of only 7·8 oz.

Experiments were made with various alloys for the head, which in the production job weighs only some 50 lb. Possibility of damage in the machine shop is overcome by taking from the final face a cut of 0·02 in. DTD424 is now used for heads, this having good machining characteristics. A high silicon alloy is not only much more expensive, but the machining characteristics generally are inferior.

Many interesting crankshaft tests were made in prototype XK engines, the shaft now being of EN16 steel, heat-treated before machining. No difficulty was experienced, as some critics had suggested, in balancing the shaft, which is simply balanced dynamically on an Avery, and the flywheel statically balanced with a Micropoise static balancer before the whole final assembly, including clutch, is re-checked statically. American Jaguar users first had an opportunity of driving the latest development of the XK engine, as used in the XK150 S. This is the 'Gold Top' version, with 9-to-1 compression ratio, developing 250 b.h.p. at 5,500 r.p.m. On test the maximum speed of the XK150 S coupé is 136 m.p.h. (218·9 k.p.h.) on overdrive top, with acceleration figures of 0–60 in 8·9 secs, and 0–120 m.p.h. in 39·5 secs. This version of the XK has now been standardized by Jaguar, and is available in United Kingdom and all oversea markets.

Claude Bailey, 'Tat' Tatersall, Bill Thornton and others such as Walter Hassan previously associated with the XK project must be proud of the unit they united to create. Their work was honoured in 1951 by the award of the Dewar Challenge Trophy. This trophy, presented to the Royal Automobile Club by Sir Thomas Dewar in 1906, is presented annually by the Club on the recommendation of the Technical and Engineering Committee for the most outstanding technical performance during the year.

In 1907 it had been awarded to Rolls-Royce for the successful 15,000-mile trial of the Silver Ghost. In 1909 it went to Daimler for the 132-hour test and 2,000-mile Brooklands endurance trial. In 1910 it went to S. F. Edge, who with the 59·9 h.p. Napier did the London to Edinburgh and back top-gear trial. And in 1951, a golden year for Jaguar, the Dewar Trophy was awarded to the company for success in four major international events, headed of course by the great Le Mans win with the C-type Jaguars, being the first time for sixteen years that a British car had been victorious.

Four

VICTORIOUS VARIANTS

ONLY once has the industrial pace of Jaguar been halted, and that was on the night of 12th February 1957 when fire swept over the huge Coventry plant, gutting a quarter of the factory and doing damage estimated at close on £3,000,000. While it was at first believed the damage would be widespread, it was confined to departments engaged in final assembly and dispatch, and hundreds of completed and partly assembled cars were destroyed.

Sir William Lyons himself worked all night among the brigades fighting desperately to limit the fire, and around dawn was approached by a newspaperman anxious to get a 'quote' on the tragedy. With his characteristic flair for convincing understatement, Sir William said: 'All our stores have gone, but tomorrow we will see what can be done.'

On the morrow two things were in fact done, one a public act of faith on Sir William's part, the other a private act of caution, details of which could not be disclosed at the time.

While the assessors and fire experts were still trying to estimate the damage among the charred remains of machine-tools, factory girders and wrecked cars, Sir William ordered the Jaguar Company flag, in orange and blue, to be hoisted over the smoke-blackened buildings. This is normally done only for celebrations and to greet Very Very Important Persons, and the assistant given the order paused for an instant to query Sir William's instruction.

'Yes, hoist the flag,' repeated Sir William. And then, with dry wit, '*Not half-mast!*'

This single gesture started a Commando-like campaign of recovery, and a vast new factory section was built *in twelve weeks*.

'I feel impelled to say now,' admitted Sir William later on, 'that the fire could hardly have come at a worse time for us, as when it occurred we were just bringing into full operation the expanded capacity of our factory, which would have enabled us to meet the very large orders in hand. I am afraid the set-back occasioned by the fire resulted in many disappointed customers throughout the world. . . . Recovery from the fire constitutes a remarkable achievement on the part of all who have been engaged on the formidable task of renewing, repairing and rehabilitating plant, buildings and machinery affected by the disaster. The principal factor in the re-establishment of our production—and indeed the factor which saved us from running at a considerable loss for many months—was the erection of a new auxiliary factory extension with an area of 80,000 square feet, which was planned and erected in the record-breaking time of 12 weeks. . . .'

Privately the Jaguar Company was disturbed by rumours rife in the industry that the fire had been the work of political or other agitators; so to settle finally the question of whether there was arson or whether the fire was a tragic accident, Dr. James Firth, one of Britain's greatest forensic scientists, was called in. Dr. Firth, then head of the Home Office forensic laboratory at Preston, Lancashire, had worked on more than 200 murder cases, but arson was his speciality, and as the leading Home Office expert he had investigated practically every big fire in the country since the war.

It took him less than twelve hours to state definitely that Jaguar's £3,000,000 fire was an accident. For obvious reasons this investigation had to be conducted under conditions of greatest secrecy, and the result was not publicized. Therefore amusing rumours, no doubt extremely irritating to the Jaguar Company, are still current that the fire was the work of Communists, of a disgruntled mechanic 'refused the chance to drive at Le Mans', that it was the work of an international syndicate paid by Detroit, to check Jaguar sales to Canada and the U.S. . . .

These stories are fiction, but the fire was fact. And one of the unhappy results was the destruction of special machine-tools installed for the full-scale production of the interesting XK variant, the XK-SS, a modified D-type Jaguar designed to sell in the United States at about $5,500. The XK-SS was the latest of these variants, the first being the C-type competition car which so distinguished itself in 1951 at Le Mans.

The C-type Jaguar has a special X frame, fully triangulated up to the point of rear suspension. At this point, incidentally, the suspension is by centre-mounted torsion bar, while front suspension is slightly modified from the XK120, and rack-and-pinion steering was used.

Features of the XK120 M were incorporated in the C-type, and 8-to-1 or 9-to-1 compression ratio was used according to fuel to be used in competitions. The flywheel was lightened, a dual exhaust system fitted, a racing-type clutch was installed, oversize S.U. carburetters were fitted, valve springs fitted designed to give bounce-free operation to 6,500 r.p.m., the camshaft lift increased from $\frac{5}{16}$-in. to $\frac{3}{8}$-in., the engine sump was deepened, main bearings were of Indium-coated lead bronze. and eventually solid-skirt pistons with racing clearances (0·006 in. on the skirt) were adopted.

The C-type was found to have a maximum speed of 141 m.p.h., with performance (through the gears) of 0–30 m.p.h. in 2 seconds, 0–60 m.p.h. in 6·6 seconds, and 0–100 m.p.h. in 16·8 seconds.

The D-type made its appearance at Le Mans in 1954. Unlike previous models, it had dry-sump lubrication. The Le Mans event in 1954 proved to be a continuous battle between Jaguar and Ferrari, and although the Italian car beat Jaguar by 89 seconds in 24 hours (and a second D-type was placed 4th), on the Index-of-Performance basis the 'D' proved superior to the Ferrari, due to its lower-swept volume. Later, at Rheims, it was the D-type which *averaged* 104·55 m.p.h.

While the frame of the C-type was tubular, with triangulation, the D-type used a centre-section of monocoque construction. The dry-sump lubrication system, enabling the engine to be placed lower owing to the very small sump, resulted in better aerodynamic lines for the whole car, and as the main part of the monocoque section was made of magnesium alloy, the all-up weight was 2,300 lb.

Front suspension was by upper and lower wishbones with torsion bars, and rear suspension was by live axle, trailing links and single transverse torsion bar. The modified XK engine, with 9-to-1 compression ratio, was mounted in the frame at an angle of 8 degrees, with the Weber carburetters horizontal. This enabled the overall height of the bonnet to be lowered, and also simplified the mounting of the engine in the complex forward structure of the magnesium-alloy frame. Dunlop disc brakes with 12¾-in. discs were used, with three pairs of pads bearing on each front disc. The 37-gallon fuel tank was in fact a double section, fuel being carried in two flexible tanks mounted within light-alloy boxes.

Mike Hawthorn and Ivor Bueb drove the winning factory D-type Jaguar in the 1955 Le Mans. A production model D-type was marketed in 1956, and performance data on this is as follows: Axle ratio 2·79. Three Weber twin-choke carburetters. Dunlop racing tyres 7·00 x 16. Performance: 0–50 m.p.h. in 3·9 seconds, 0–60 m.p.h., 4·7 seconds, 0–100 m.p.h., 12·1 seconds. Standing quarter-mile, 13·7 seconds, and maximum rated speed 162 m.p.h.

While development was continuing through the years on the standard XK C- and D-types, a number of other variants such as the HWM-Jaguar, Lister-Jaguar and Tojeiro-Jaguar were winning laurels.

Initial success of the HWM was obtained with a special chassis and an Alta engine, and the first 3½-litre car with the XK engine made its appearance in the 1954 *Daily Express* Silverstone meeting, with George Abecassis driving. He finished second to Gonzalez in the big 4·9-litre Ferrari.

HWM was the combination of George Abecassis (the present managing director of H.W. Motors Ltd.) and John Heath. They had both been actively interested in racing for many years, and their partnership in the prosperous motor business at Hersham and Walton gave rise to the racing HWM, named after the initials of the company. Heath and Abecassis designed a tubular racing frame, with transverse leaf-spring-and-wishbone front suspension, and transverse leaf-spring at rear. The design was first on the board in 1948, when the only suitable power unit was the 2-litre Alta. Heath and Abecassis had already had racing success with it, and the first true HWM made its appearance at the Easter meeting at Goodwood in 1949.

During its first season the HWM, with John Heath at the wheel, was victorious at the Isle of Man, and a team of three cars was built during the autumn and winter months. As this was really a spare-time venture, a part-time welder was engaged, evenings only! In view of the subsequent success of Abecassis and Heath it is amusing to recall the small beginnings of the HWM. They arranged to drive one car each, and a professional driver was to be engaged for the third of the 'team' cars.

Stirling Moss, who had raced against Heath in the B.R.D.C. Manx Cup event and made a great name for himself in the '500' class and with the Cooper '1000', was signed up. Moss sold his Cooper just after his twentieth birthday, and became a member of the HWM team.

All through the summer of 1950 the team raced the Alta-engined HWM, at Rheims, Naples, Mons, Aix-le-Bains, and then back home at Silverstone. The HWM certainly gave Moss his first big chance, and also incidentally it led to his being appointed to the Jaguar works team. At the end of the Silverstone event, Moss was approached by Tommy Wisdom and invited to drive the XK120 in the T.T.

'Wisdom's offer of his Jaguar sports car,' relates Stirling Moss in his *Book of Motor Sport*, 'became in my racing career one of those turning-point opportunities which, with a bit of luck, comes to every young man. The three-hour T.T. race up in the hills at Dundrod, near Belfast, was held in a driving storm of wind and rain. . . . Everything was soaked, and the daytime visibility became so atrocious that one team drove with sidelights.

After averaging 76·2 m.p.h. for 2½ hours I saw my father's signal to go all out for the last slithery lap. I swallowed another mouthful of rainwater, kept my foot down and managed a new T.T. lap record of 77·61 m.p.h. Altogether, in the process of winning the race for Tommy Wisdom, I had covered 225 miles non-stop. My gratitude to Wisdom was heartfelt, for this wet and wonderful day at Dundrod led directly to my joining the Jaguar team in 1951. Many miles, many cars and many millions of r.p.m. later, I became No. 1 Jaguar driver. . . .'

The HWM team enjoyed many successes after Moss joined Jaguar, but for a considerable time they stayed faithful to the

Alta engine, modified by Milledge and R. R. Jackson, and a smart aluminium body was used, built by Leacroft of Egham. Lance Macklin, Peter Collins and other brilliant drivers raced various versions of the HWM, and in the 1953 car the Alta engine was used with a Jaguar gearbox. At the hands of Abecassis, the Jaguar-engined HWM made its debut, and at Rheims (12-hours) the HWM-Jaguar driven by Tony Gaze and Graham Whitehead came seventh to the works Jaguars. In 1954, too, Abecassis showed a fine pace at Hyères, lying second for most of the event, and the car also made a good appearance at Dundrod in the same year.

Abecassis' famous 'HWM-1' has a tubular frame, whereas later production models are much modified. Helical springs were later used, and there has been much weight-saving. The Jaguar Company made many D-type engines available for the HWM, and the final version was an excellent dual-purpose vehicle for competition work and ordinary road motoring. Maximum speed of the HWM-Jaguar is around 145 m.p.h., and a test shows that the standing quarter-mile can be covered in 15 seconds. The time for 0–100 m.p.h. with this ultra-lightweight 17 cwt. Jaguar is approximately 17 seconds.

The HWM team became the proving-ground of many famous men in the Jaguar world. Apart from giving Stirling Moss his first big opportunity for Continental racing, the HWM racing department has been the starting-point for Alf Francis (later famous for his work with Moss' cars), Len Hayden, who joined the Jaguar racing division, and Frank Webb who ultimately became chief development engineer with Harry Weslake, the concern responsible for much initial work connected with porting and cylinder-head design of the XK engine.

The Tojeiro-Jaguar is produced by J. M. Tojeiro, and Tojeiro Automotive Developments Ltd now have extensive works at Barkway, near Royston, Hertfordshire. Prototype racing Tojeiro-Jaguars were produced at the Byfleet works. One of the most celebrated T.-J.s is owned by the Ecurie Ecosse, and the *marque* has a string of successes including, most recently, 2nd place in the Unlimited Sports Car Race at the July Silverstone Grand Prix meeting (1958), and 1st with the lap record at the Charterhall Closed meeting.

On the eve of the Mille Miglia, 1957. W. E. 'Wilkie' Wilkinson (dark glasses) and Ron Flockhart (*right*) of the Ecurie Ecosse team, try out their Lister-Jaguar, and meet Stirling Moss and Denis Jenkinson (*Motor Sport* Continental Correspondent) trying out the course in their 4·5-litre Maserati

Jaguar driver J. Duncan Hamilton (*right*) greets Mille Miglia and Targa Floria veteran, Piero Taruffi, on the eve of the Oporto (Portugal) Grand Prix—the event in which Hamilton sustained serious injuries, breaking his neck, jaw and nine ribs

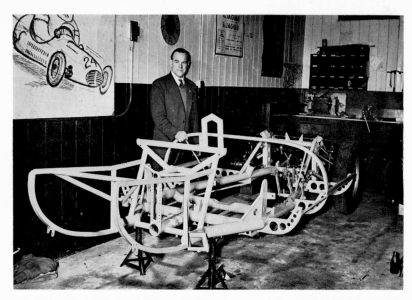

W. E. 'Wilkie' Wilkinson checks the first Lister chassis supplied for the Ecurie Ecosse. This was supplied in kit form, and built up by the Ecurie mechanics at Merchiston Mews. It will be noted that this Lister has the slide for the rear axle, whereas the Tojeiro uses Watts linkage

Prototype body for the first Lister-Jaguar designed for the Ecurie Ecosse. This is the rough sketch of the car used for basis of discussions between Brian Lister and David Murray. Subsequently, many modifications were made, including scrapping of the bench-type seat

Latest production car in this series is the Tojeiro-Jaguar Mk. IV, which can be supplied fitted with any of the twin o.h.c. engines from the 3-litre to the 3·8, and fitted with either a close-ratio C- or D-type gearbox. The chassis frame is of the multitubular space-frame type, using $1\frac{5}{8}$-in. main members, and $1\frac{1}{4}$-in., 1-in. and $\frac{5}{8}$-in. secondary members, built in 18 s.w.g. mild-steel tubing. This frame is rigid, and includes all mountings for engine, gearbox, front and rear suspension, final-drive assembly, as well as brackets for clutch, brake and throttle pedals, etc. Total weight of the stripped frame is only 88 lb.

Front suspension is by unequal wishbones, the springing medium being helical springs around Armstrong adjustable damper units, while the rear suspension is of the De Dion type. This uses parallel trailing links for fore-and-aft location, and a Watts linkage for lateral location. The beam is fabricated from 3-in. 14 s.w.g. mild-steel tube, and is integral with the rear hub carriers. Springing is by helical springs around Armstrong dampers, as at the front.

Brakes of the Mk. IV are Girling disc at front, with C-type light alloy calliper acting on centrifugally cast iron discs of 12-in. diameter. These are mounted outboard at the front on the hubs, and inboard at the rear on the final-drive unit. Front and rear systems are entirely independent, having separate master cylinders which are linked by a bias-bar so that the front-to-rear ratio can be varied to suit individual drivers.

Steering is by lightweight rack-and-pinion assembly. The steering column has adjustable rake. Final-drive arrangements can be supplied to suit driver's own preference. The Mk. IV is normally fitted with a Salisbury 4 HU unit which incorporates either a power-lock limited-slip differential as standard equipment, or a ZF limited-slip differential as optional equipment. Ratios available range from 2·93 to 4·09.

J. M. Tojeiro has designed a special final drive which is also available as an alternative on the Mk. IV. This is a quick-change unit incorporating a Ford crown-wheel and pinion of ZF limited-slip differential, and has a low input shaft giving a much lower propeller-shaft line. This unit is patterned on the American Halibrand unit, and offers an exceptional range and combination of final drive.

As standard equipment the car is fitted with Dunlop light-alloy disc-type peg-drive centre-lock wheels, fitted with 600 by 16 tyres at the front and 650 by 16 at the rear. Dunlop R3 or R5 pattern are available.

Bodywork of the Mk. IV is interesting, being a full-width two-seater complying with FIA Appendix C, and having all wheels enclosed. Headlamps are recessed behind Perspex covers. Front and rear halves of the body are quickly detachable, and when these are removed work can easily be done on engine and final drive. Height at scuttle is only 29 in. The complete Mk. IV was listed in 1959 at £2,050 ex works, and it is also supplied, in kit form, to many famous racing units such as the Ecurie Ecosse.

It was, oddly enough, a Tojeiro chassis which first introduced the designer of another victorious Jaguar variant to success in car racing. Young Brian Lister became interested in cars in 1946 during the time when he was an A.C.2 in the Royal Air Force. He had by then completed two years' apprenticeship with his father's engineering concern in Cambridge, and to while away the boredom of an isolated airfield in Wales he bought and tinkered with a number of sports cars including a TA-type M.G., and a Morgan 4–4. He fitted an M.G. engine to a Cooper chassis, and in 1951 began driving a Tojeiro chassis powered by an air-cooled J.A.P. engine.

At the end of that season Archie Scott Brown was beginning to show his abilities as a racing driver, and Brian Lister invited him to team up with another Cambridge engineer, Don Moore, whose speciality was the tuning of racing engines and who himself had won some fifty sprints and races in four years. Mr. Lister, senior, offered to back them on the understanding that he would review their success after eighteen months. Few could foretell how great that success would be.

Their first project, the Lister-M.G., was little more than a test-bed for their theories, but Archie Scott Brown was so impressed with the car's ability that they decided to purchase a Bristol engine. The following season the Lister-Bristol won its class in the Sports Car Race at the Silverstone Grand Prix meeting, and orders for production models began to flow in. During 1956 a great deal of time was spent developing a Lister-

Maserati, but racing results were disappointing, largely owing to faults arising from defective materials in the power-unit. The camshaft had to be chromium-plated to combat wear, there were instances of valve fracture, and of broken teeth in the timing. Eventually an XK D-type Jaguar engine was available, and its much greater power and reliability proved the making of the Lister concern. By 1957 this car was so developed that Archie Scott Brown enjoyed a lengthy list of successes, including eleven firsts in the fourteen races he entered. And in each case he equalled or bettered the existing lap record for sports cars.

Outstanding successes of the Lister-Jaguar include: *1957*: B.R.D.C. British Empire Trophy, Oulton Park; B.A.R.C. International, Goodwood; W.E.C.C. Sprint, Snetterton; B.R.S.C.C., Crystal Palace; B.A.R.C.-R.A.C. International, Aintree; M.G.C.C., Silverstone; B.R.D.C., Silverstone, and B.A.R.C. National, Goodwood. *1959*: Levin, New Zealand International; B.R.D.C. British Empire Trophy, Oulton Park; B.A.R.C. International, Aintree; B.R.D.C. International, Silverstone; B.R.S.C.C., Mallory Park; B.A.R.C., Goodwood; B.R.D.A.C., Silverstone, and many more.

A road-test of the production Lister-Jaguar, with the 10–to–1 compression ratio engine and three Weber carburetters, gave the standing quarter-mile in 13·2 seconds, maximum speed 140 m.p.h. and more, according to final-gear ratio, and acceleration 0–100 m.p.h. in 11·2 seconds.

In an extensive road-test, conducted by John Bolster for *Autosport* in October 1957, he praised the sports-touring merits of the Lister-Jaguar after Archie Scott Brown had proved its worth as Britain's fastest sports-racing car.

'I still feel, however,' remarked Bolster, 'that the landlord of my local pub summed it up perfectly. "One moment he was here," he said, "and the next moment he wasn't!" '

That is certainly the acme of acceleration with any Jaguar variant.

For 1959 a new aerodynamic body is used on Lister-Jaguar, designed by Frank Costin who joined the Company as chief designer. As is to be expected, there are similarities with Costin's bodies for Lotus, which have already proved their aerodynamic and low-drag qualities. A new development in engine-mounting has removed the slight hump in the bonnet, and there is ingenious air ducting, making use of the cockpit air depression experienced at speed.

Dunlop disc brakes and centre-lock alloy wheels are now used, and the inboard rear disc brakes are cooled in somewhat similar manner to the Vanwall. The works team for 1959 included Ivor Bueb and Bruce Halford, and arrangements made by Briggs Cunningham and others to race the car internationally should add still more laurels to the Cambridge Lister-Jaguar team.

Five

D.M. AND E.E.

E.E. stands for Ecurie Ecosse, the most successful private racing stable. D.M. is its patron, David Murray.

Most people—even those who do not own or support the *marque* of Jaguar—know that the near-fabulous Ecurie Ecosse has been the chief exponent of the Jaguar and has set a long line of milestones on motor-racing history. Few, however, realize how intensive these victories have been, or what a tribute the entire venture is to David Murray.

What established the distinguished position of the E.E. were the fine lists of victories gained in the first five years of its existence. They are as follows:

1952. In its first year the E.E. entered 18 events, and it had outright or class wins in 13 of them. The victories were at Turnberry (three times), Isle of Man, Jersey (twice), Charterhall (three times), Crimond, Goodwood, Castle Coombe, and the Wakefield Trophy.

1953. There were 16 entries, and victories at Charterhall, Ibsley, Castle Coombe, Thruxton (twice), Rheims, Snetterton (three times), Spa and Nürburgring.

1954. Again 18 entries, with outright or class wins at: Buenos Aires, Goodwood (five times), Ibsley, Silverstone, Snetterton, Oulton Park, Charterhall (twice), and Zandvoort, Holland. In this season the E.E. cars broke six lap records.

1955. Nine entries, but the average of victories went up. Ulster, Leinster, Charterhall, Snetterton, Goodwood and Crimond (twice).

1956. The entries were back to 15, including the final great victory at Le Mans, and the E.E. established its success beyond doubt: Snetterton, Goodwood (three times), Oulton Park, Charterhall (twice), Spa, Silverstone, and Le Mans.

Subsequent successes of the E.E. team will be fresh in memory, and the 1957 Le Mans victory was a Jaguar and E.E. triumph. Jaguars came in first, second, third, fourth and sixth. This was the first time in Le Mans history that one make took the first four places—a triumph which Bentley, Bugatti, Lagonda, Mercedes and others with all their glory had never succeeded in achieving. And the first two cars were those of the E.E.—Ivor Bueb and Ron Flockhart in the winning Jaguar, 113·85 m.p.h., followed by Ninian Sanderson and John Lawrence, 111·05 m.p.h.

The success-story of the E.E. began with a lucky accident. David Murray first became known as a racing motorist in the early post-war years. This genial Edinburgh figure—in private life an accountant, and the head of a group of companies dealing in Scotch whisky—was frequently to be found racing a Maserati attached to the Parnell stable, and subsequently at the wheel of his own Maserati.

In 1951 D.M. entered his car for the German Grand Prix at the Nürburgring, and during practice on the twisty circuit, on the last run before the Grand Prix itself, D.M. ran out of road and sped through a stand of sturdy fir trees. The Maserati was almost a complete write-off, and D.M. was lucky to escape with his life. Jenny Murray used the arguments that so many other wives of racing men have done, but as D.M. had racing in his blood it was a natural step to develop a motor-racing team for others.

D.M., always modest about his own achievements, likes to joke that 'I only started a garage business to get my racing bits at trade discount. I'm a Scot. . . .' In fact his organization, Merchiston Motors, is one of the most experienced suppliers and distributors of sports and racing cars, and the technical facilities of his company have been put completely at the disposal of the Ecurie Ecosse, which was formed in December 1951.

D.M. was fortunate in securing the services of 'W.W.'— W. E. Wilkinson, the famous racing expert, driver and designer.

'Wilkie' Wilkinson started racing in 1928 when he joined the O.M. concern, and raced with R. F. Oats. Two years later he became travelling mechanic to Ramponi (O.M.), in the Ulster T.T., and in 1931 accompanied Oats and Widengren (Maserati) in the Brooklands Double-Twelve, George Eyston (Maserati) in the Irish Grand Prix, and Widengren (Maserati) in the T.T.

In 1932 he joined Dennis and Kenneth Evans in the Belle-vue Garage, Wandsworth, as works manager, and his debut as a racing driver came when he drove Ken's Montlhery M.G. Midget to victory in the Lewes Speed Trials. At Brooklands he scored many victories with the Bellevue M.G.s, became director of the organization in 1937, and at that period he was often to be found racing with drivers such as Billy Cotton, the bandleader of 'Wakey, Wakey' fame. Wilkie and Billy took third place in 1937 with Cotton's M.G. in the J.C.C. International Trophy Race, and the following year Billy and Wilkie in an E.R.A. secured third place in the British Empire Trophy.

During the war, Wilkie was in charge of Rotol's test hangar at Cheltenham, and he returned to racing in 1947, flying to Sweden to prepare Reg Parnell's E.R.A. For the next two years he used his expert 'tuning fork' on various racing cars for Parnell, David Murray and the Ashmore brothers, and when D.M. outlined the ambitious plan for the Ecurie Ecosse, following the accident at the Nürburgring, Wilkie was swept away with enthusiasm. This, in brief, is the pen-picture of the man who has brought the E.E. Jaguars to a pitch of technical excellence.

'When the team was formed in December 1951,' D.M. told me, 'our first and—characteristically—our only organized meeting was attended by the drivers Sir James Scott-Douglas, Ian Stewart and Bill Dobson, by "Wilkie", by Reg Tanner the racing manager of Esso, and by myself. At the outset I had estimated that three years would be the proving time of the Ecurie Ecosse. If at the end of that time the team was either not good enough to compete in international events, or that financially it was impossible to continue, so it must be, and I would call it a day.'

W. A. 'Bill' Dobson, one of the original team, throws an amusing light on the initial efforts of the E.E.

'During my connection with the team as driver,' he told me, 'I was asked many, many times what "Ecurie Ecosse" meant. When I replied "Scottish Stable", the results were varied—from "*Oh yes, I see*" to blank looks of uncertainty as to how a Scottish Stable could have any connection with the steel-blue Jaguars. I soon had the impression that a lot of English and Continental people conjured up in their mind's eye a vision of a Scottish Stable built of grey stone, with heather growing all over the place!

'A favourite expression in the christening year of the Ecurie Ecosse was "The Haggis Bashers". This name was devised by the amiable racing driver Cliff Davies, and it has stuck. It was up to us to prove that we could bash more than haggis. We also bashed our Jaguars.

'The cars we had in the first year were immaculately turned out, but I think Wilkie will be the first to admit that they could not have done a trouble-free 24-hour run at Le Mans, as we did later with the D-type. The disc brakes of the D can stand the strain of long and hard braking, which those on our first Jaguars could not. The rather ineffective brakes (under racing conditions) on the first Jaguars were a constant source of worry not only to Wilkie, who had to keep producing linings from all sources, but to us who drove the cars.

'During the first year, by the time we arrived at Castle Coombe, Wilkie had devised three air vents to each wheel to draw cool air on the brake-drums. However, Mother Nature took a hand, and completely upset Wilkie's calculations by producing a bright, cloudless day which would have done credit to a Mediterranean motor course.

'So during the entire practice period and after every race the routine was the same: wheels off—drums off—fresh linings on—drums on again (if they were not cracked due to heat), and then an argument as to whether the air vents should face forward or to the rear, as we all had different ideas as to which way gave us better braking. Well, they were the pioneering days of trial for Wilkie and all connected with the E.E. . . .'

The Ecurie Ecosse is full of personalities who blend into a most efficient and happy team under D.M.'s banner, and Reg Tanner, competitions manager of the Esso Petroleum Company, has mothered the team through many of its financial difficulties. Some of his protégés in other spheres have been Dick Seaman, Stirling Moss, Mike Hawthorn, Roy Salvadori and of course many individual members of the E.E. team.

'Every member is tremendously enthusiastic and has a keen sense of responsibility,' he told me, 'but sometimes this is hidden behind a gay or carefree exterior. Not so, however, with Ian Stewart who was an early member of the Ecurie. I remember how he used to get so worked up before a race-meeting that he was a bundle of nerves by the time the flag fell. In Jersey, in 1951, he will doubtless remember that my colleague, Geoff Murdoch, and I spent an entire morning trying to divert his thoughts from the afternoon's race. I don't think I have ever talked for so long on the subject of cattle, or drunk so much coffee! But it proved worth while, for Ian won his race convincingly.

'Bill Dobson, on the other hand, seemed to have no cares or worries at all. Whatever happened, we always knew that Bill would cross the finishing line safely and be in his office by Monday. He was quite imperturbable. Ninian Sanderson is good company, and unpredictable! I often imagine his tolerant wife welcoming him home one minute, only to be told that he is off to the Continent for a Grand Prix race the next minute. I am sure she is one of the many "motor-racing wives" glad to pack her husband's bags so that she can get on with her chores and bringing up the children! Jimmy Stewart was a grand personality, always smiling and confident. Somehow he always managed to get leave for motor-racing during his National Service, and I was never able to discover if he had an exceptionally understanding C.O., or if this was just Jimmy's good-natured way of getting round people!'

Jimmy Stewart, now a partner with his father in an engineering business at Bowling, told me: 'I always recall the first time I saw the three blue-painted Jaguars, at a race-meeting at Charterhall. When the main Sports Car Race was about to start, the potent Jaguars were positioned on the starting-grid near my own Healey "Silverstone". Then the flag was lowered, and in less than a lap I could see them no more. They had just shot out of my vision, and I was quite disgruntled at being made to look so slow!

'Later I was asked by "D.M." if I would be interested in

signing up for the 1953 racing season with the Ecurie. There was one main snag—I was serving in the R.E.M.E. as a driving instructor. However, my C.O. allowed me leave when duties permitted.

'That season I was to race in Germany. Many times I had seen films and read about the famous Nürburgring circuit; it is stupendous, consisting of acute right- and left-hand turns.

'On this circuit there is the famous corner known as the Carousel. This turn is banked considerably, the approach to the bend being fairly steep. Consequently the road seems to subside, and you realize the Carousel is in control! The car seems to take over, or perhaps it is the acute banking of the Carousel. It is certainly a thrilling and unique experience.

'This particular event was the 1,000-km. Sports Car Race, and my team-mate was John Lawrence, of Cullen. I shall never forget those practice sessions, as we found it most difficult to memorize the twisting course. In fact I can still admit I have not a full idea of the quickest way round. John and I, however, had the good fortune to finish sixth in the general classification, and second in the class, even though that Jaguar was somewhat battered around. . . .

'The 1954 season started with an invitation to compete in the 1,000-km. Sports Car Race at Buenos Aires. Jenny Murray, Wilkie, Ninian Sanderson and I travelled by air, "D.M." escorted the cars by sea, and Ian Stewart and Sir James Scott-Douglas were already in South America awaiting our arrival.

'I was co-driving with Ian Stewart and unfortunately, when he was lying very well placed in the race, he became involved with two Porsches, and was forced off the road. Fortunately he was not seriously hurt, but this was a very unlucky trip for me, as after travelling such a long way I did not even race. That's motor-racing!'

E.E. drivers at various times have included Ian Stewart, Scott-Douglas, Jimmy Stewart, Bill Dobson, Ninian Sanderson, Desmond Titterington, John Lawrence, Alan Brown, Ron Flockhart, Jack Fairman, Ivor Bueb, Innes Ireland and Masten Gregory. First secretary of the team was Eve Southwood, later leaving to join Laurence Pomeroy, and Wendy Jones has now been D.M.'s secretary since 1956.

D.M. uses a pocket-size wire-recorder to record urgent

instructions in connection with the E.E., and this has over-come previous difficulties of deciphering handwriting! Wendy helps to book all arrangements for the team's international journeys, keeps the Press cuttings-books up to date, deals with staff matters, acts as liaison between the drivers, the mechanics and D.M. himself, and in fact attends to most behind-the-scenes administrative details of the Ecurie—except attending races! The E.E. organization necessitates her staying at 'The Mews' when the racing team goes out, so even at the height of excitement, such as Le Mans, Miss Jones has to keep herself informed of what 'her' team is doing simply through the commentaries of Raymond Baxter and others.

Wilkie Wilkinson, known to the E.E. team as 'the Laird of Merchiston', has a gift for making machinery go faster than even its makers intended, and the story is told that he once spent five minutes repairing his neighbour's lawn-mower, then worked on the engine for three hours trying to make it run faster! The 'Wilkie-ized' XK120's were successful at Charter-hall on 6th April 1952, followed by encouraging results at Castle Coombe and in the Isle of Man, so a C-type was ordered for Jersey, where of course the Ecurie had its first international victory.

'We knew what we were getting into right from the begin-ning,' said D.M., who had made a shoe-string assault on the viciously competitive international sports-car world, 'and we made up our minds that no Ecurie Ecosse car was ever going to start a race it did not have a chance of winning.'

On one occasion at the Nürburgring circuit, the tight turns and the high speed of the tuned XK120 imposed more stress than the standard wheels were designed to take. One by one they showed sign of collapse, and Wilkie became worried that this unpredicted weakness would lose any chance of victory. Then, the resourceful 'Laird' looked at the back of the pits and saw D.M.'s own Mk. VII Jaguar parked there. One by one the wheels were stripped off, and by the time the XK120 was successfully crossing the finishing line, D.M.'s Mk. VII was on jacks.

To this day D.M. regrets accepting a subsequent invitation to enter the E.E. team at the Nürburgring—such an unlucky circuit for him personally—as in this event two of the three blue E.E. Jaguars crashed. Titterington and Jimmy Stewart spent some time in hospital, and Jimmy subsequently retired from motor-racing to concentrate on the family engineering business.

Seconds count in racing, as the E.E. realized bitterly on one occasion in the 1955 season. During the nine-hour event at Goodwood, the single Ecurie entry had to spend $3\frac{1}{2}$ minutes in the pits while a broken headlamp was repaired, and as a result the Jaguar finished second, losing to a works Aston-Martin by only 21 seconds. In the winter of 1955–6 Wilkie, aided by his mechanics Ron Gaudion, Stan Sproat and Pat Meehan, rebuilt the two cars so badly crashed in Germany, and the decision was taken to try the luck of the Ecurie at Le Mans.

The Jaguar works team of Hawthorn/Bueb, Frère/Titterington and Fairman/Wharton was entered and two of the three works Jags were Lucas fuel-injected. Three works Aston-Martins were also entered, with such formidable drivers as Stirling Moss, Peter Collins, Walker, Salvadori, Parnell and Brooks. In addition, there were dangerous entries by Ferrari, Talbot-Maserati and Porsche.

The starter's flag fell, and so did the rain. For 20 of the 24 hours the Sarthe circuit was one of the wettest ever, and some of the disasters happened in the first ten minutes. Frère spun on the glistening wet road when taking his D-type into the esses, and Fairman, following close on his tail, did the same. Portago's Ferrari crashed into both cars, leaving the Jaguar works team with only one car left after the first ten minutes of the 24-hour marathon. To add to 'Lofty' England's troubles, Hawthorn brought the remaining car into the pits with suspected fuel-injection trouble, and nearly an hour was spent in checking the system until at last it was found that a defect not directly connected with the Lucas pump-and-shuttle system was the cause of the trouble. This undoubtedly cost Hawthorn the race.

Stirling Moss in the Aston was still running well, but the speed and reliability of Ron Flockhart and Ninian Sanderson —driving the rebuilt car which Stewart had mangled so badly at the Nürburgring the preceding year—was remarkable, and by the 12-hour mark Flockhart was back in the lead, never to be seriously challenged for the rest of the race. Stirling put on speed after midday when the course began to dry out a little,

but was still nearly 10 miles behind the winning E.E. Jaguar
when the chequered flag fell. In this gruelling event the rain had
taken its toll, and 28 cars were involved in accidents more or
less directly arising from the bad surface conditions, and only
14 cars finished. The Ecurie Ecosse had entered one car, and it
won. . . .

At the end of the 1956 season the Jaguar Company announced
that they would not at that time be entering a works team in
international competition, and D.M. was invited to acquire the
works team of D-types. Generously he agreed to provide the
necessary capital and facilities, and the famous cars were
transported to join the others in 'The Mews'. That season had
a poor start, as Flockhart tried to ram a tree at Buenos Aires,
although Ninian Sanderson and Roberto Mieres finished
fourth overall in the other E.E.-entered Jaguar.

For the 1956 Le Mans the E.E. faced very stiff competition,
for Ferrari had Collins, Hill, Hawthorn and Trintignant, while
Maserati signed Stirling Moss, Schell, Behra, Fangio and
others. The Maserati team, incidentally, were using the
Sebring 4·5 with a body designed by Frank Costin, now of
Lister-Jaguar. Aston-Martin drivers included Brooks, Les
Leston, the Whitehead brothers, Salvadori and Cunningham-
Reid. During practice, timing showed that the 3·8 fuel-
injected E.E. Jaguars were lapping at rather lower speeds than
some of D.M.'s rivals, and Gregor Grant asked Murray how
he felt about this inferior speed during the few practice
laps.

'What you do in two, or ten, laps at Le Mans doesn't make
much difference,' smiled D.M. 'It's what you do in twenty-
four hours that counts.'

The story of that particular Le Mans marathon is one of
clockwork-like regularity, for the winning car of Ron Flockhart
and Ivor Bueb soon assumed the lead, and ran with trouble-
free ·throughout the 2,732 miles covered in the twenty-
four hours. Tony Brooks' Aston hit a sandbank at Tetre
Rouge, and Maglioli's Porsche was also out of the running soon
after dawn on the Sunday. From that moment the Sanderson-
Lawrence Jaguar moved up to second place, and held it. Not
content with this fantastic success—the first time two privately
owned Jaguars had been successful at Le Mans—D.M. and

Wilkie took their team across to Monza the following week-end, where the cars finished fourth, fifth and sixth (Fairman, Sanderson and Lawrence) despite the unfair contest which one columnist described as a 'David (Murray)-and-Goliath contest' against the crack Indianapolis single-seater racing cars.

Subsequently D.M. put the three D-types up for sale, and made plans to concentrate on racing light, independent chassis such as Lister and Tojeiro, and in common with 'Laird' Wilkie he pins his faith in future mechanical progress of cars for the Ecurie in the good old Scots phrase 'Guid gear comes in sma' buik'.

Since running up this long string of victories, with Le Mans in 1956 and 1957, the E.E. has no intention of resting on its laurels, and one of the problems in D.M.'s mind is that more capital and bigger racing and technical resources must be found. Sports-loving motorists the world over have been inspired by the Ecurie's victories against powerful international works teams, and they have asked how they can be associated with the most successful private racing stable of all time.

An answer, in part, has been found by the formation of the Ecurie Ecosse Association, which not only affords its members an opportunity of associating themselves with the venture but which in time may also provide funds to purchase cars and equipment, and to enable a future generation of skilled racing drivers to be entered in international events. Membership of the Ecurie Ecosse Association (fee £2), Associate Membership and Junior Membership are open to all, and full members are eligible to vote in the management of the Association, to take office on the committee and so to help to ensure a continuing future for E.E. Application for membership of the Association should be made direct to the Secretary of the Ecurie Ecosse Association Ltd., 7 Merchiston Mews, Edinburgh, 10. A monthly magazine is issued free to subscribers. The Hon. President of the Association is Lord Bruce.

Six

BRAKES, TYRES—AND LAURELS

'IN recognition of the great contribution made by the disc
brake to safety and efficiency,' said Sir William Lyons in
June 1958, 'the Dunlop Company has been awarded the Dewar
Trophy. . . . We ourselves, in the past, have been privileged to
hold this trophy' (*see* page 54) 'and I congratulate the Dunlop
Company on the recognition accorded them. . . .'

Modestly, he did not mention that Jaguar and Dunlop
were 'partners in power' since 1951, when facilities were given
to the Jaguar concern for testing a number of prototype
Dunlop disc-brake systems. H. J. Butler (design) and Harry
Hodkinson and A. J. Holloway of Dunlops were entrusted with
the task of developing this new brake for a Jaguar racing car.
The brake tried in 1952 showed some success, but on the really
brake-punishing circuits serious faults showed up. The team
went back to their drawing-board.

Throughout the winter of 1952–3 a pale-blue Jaguar was
used for extensive trials at Lindley, and the Dunlop team had
to take anti-sickness tablets to cure the effects caused by repeated acceleration to more than 100 m.p.h., crash-braking,
then accelerating again, each cycle taking less than a minute.

Eventually a disc-brake system suitable for racing was
produced by Butler and Hodkinson, and, as we shall see,
Stirling Moss won the first of a famous series of races on the
very fast circuit at Rheims in a C-type Jaguar fitted with disc
brakes, and the following year disc-braked Jaguars were
victorious at Le Mans and in the Rheims 12-hour race. In the
succeeding years up to 1956, Jaguars were again successful at
Sebring, Rheims and Le Mans, and throughout this period of
development data was being collected by the Jaguar and
Dunlop teams.

The disc-brake development story began in 1902, when Dr.

Fred Lanchester and later a number of American engineers had developments in hand for a brake based on the idea of a clutch, in which one or more plates were gripped between layers of friction material. This layout had the advantage that a larger braking area could be provided for a given weight, but other difficulties such as cooling were as great as ever. This position was not substantially changed until Dunlops took out their patent for a disc brake of a different kind.

The essence of this is that pads of friction material of relatively small area on both sides of a disc are brought by associated hydraulic mechanism into frictional contact with the disc. This is of considerable area, so that the very moment the rotating mass of metal emerges from contact with the pads the surface is cooled by air contact. On the other hand, in the normal brake-drum, the heat is generated on the inside of the drum, and must be conducted through the thickness of the metal before any appreciable air cooling can take place.

First tests of disc brakes were made with aircraft. This was a natural step for Dunlop, who had made aircraft tyres since 1910, and then began building wheels as well, first of all wire-spoked, and, after 1929, of light alloy disc construction riveted to rims and fabricated or cast hubs with phosphor-bronze bushes. The first 'air brakes' were pneumatic devices, containing an inflatable rubber tube which pressed segments of friction material against a drum (roughly, a hydraulic-brake system, but worked pneumatically), and this was first demonstrated on an Avro Avion in 1932. Subsequently, both air and hydraulically operated bag-type brakes were featured on aircraft.

War-time developments resulted in landing wheels becoming much smaller (owing to the restricted space available for retraction), and as landing speeds and all-up weights were continually increasing, it was no longer possible to absorb so much heat without risk of the temperature rise seriously damaging tyres. As a result, Dunlop research teams worked on various ways of dissipating braking heat quickly, and in 1945 the company patented a brake in which a steel drum was replaced by metal rings keyed into and rotating with the wheel. From this design the multi-disc aircraft brake was developed. It was a natural marketing step to apply the same idea to motor-cars, but here the problems are much more difficult.

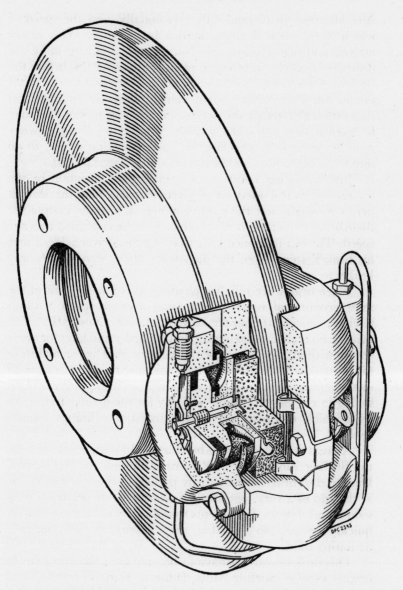

Sectioned view of front disc brake, Dunlop Mk. 2

Aircraft come in to land only occasionally, and the speed at which they touch down is known in advance. With heavy aircraft and high landing speeds a great deal of heat has to be dissipated quickly, but there is plenty of time for this before the brakes are required again, except for manœuvring at low speed on the runway. With a road vehicle, however, it is almost impossible to forecast the reserve of stopping power that may be needed in a car when a driver is hurrying along a twisty road, for constantly checking his speed from 90 m.p.h. to 30 m.p.h. among convoys of lorries on a busy arterial road.

Just as driving habits show considerable variation in the amount of petrol used on a given journey, and the slowest driver is usually not the most economical, so some people use their brakes much more than others to achieve a good average speed. The old-fashioned idea that 'a good driver seldom uses his brakes' stems from the days when there were hardly any brakes to use.

When brakes are reliable, plentiful use of them is one of the most economical ways of increasing average speed without having to accelerate harder, or cruise faster. Conversely, a fast driver who realizes he can safely brake harder and later for every corner without risk of brake-fade, will soon find he can maintain his normal average speed without opening the throttle so wide or taking his engine revolutions so high, in indirect gears. This saving in engine wear alone will pay for the greater frequency with which the relatively inexpensive brake linings require renewal.

A great deal was learned by Harold Hodkinson's team from the Stirling Moss entry at Rheims. Although these prototype Dunlop disc brakes satisfactorily pulled up the 150-m.p.h. car at the end of a very long straight once or twice per lap, it was soon found that on short events round twisty circuits the brakes quickly became so hot that they vaporized the hydraulic actuating fluid.

This rather erratic behaviour became an embarrassment to drivers such as Stirling Moss, Duncan Hamilton and others who were driving Jaguars with these brakes, but it was overcome by mounting the hydraulic cylinders on relatively slender pillars which do not transmit heat so readily. Also a rather smaller area of contact was arranged between the actuating piston and the brake-pad carrier. At the same time, a retraction device was developed by Dunlop, and with this the pads are withdrawn by springs for a distance of about 0·01 in. from the surface of the discs whenever the hydraulic pressure is released.

The use of tight-fitting bushes on the retractor pins causes these to be gripped tightly enough when the springs push back against the retractor sleeves, but the hydraulic pressure can still force the pins forward whenever the sleeves come up against their seats. The brakes are therefore self-adjusting throughout the life of the pads, as a little extra fluid enters at the master cylinder each time the pistons work themselves further up the wheel cylinders.

After the first Rheims success with Jaguar and the Dunlop prototype, the decision was made to fit discs to the C-type Jags for Le Mans in 1953, in which, as is well known, the *marque* was first, second and fourth, Tony Rolt and Duncan Hamilton winning at an average speed of over 100 m.p.h. for the first time in the history of the race. The increase in speed compared with 1952 was more than 9 m.p.h., and much of the credit was openly ascribed to the use of disc brakes.

Stirling Moss, with Peter Whitehead co-driving, won the Sports Car Race at Rheims that year. Rolt and Hamilton were second at Le Mans in 1954, and another disc-braked Jaguar driven by Peter Whitehead and Ken Wharton won the Rheims event, with Rolt and Hamilton again second.

Jaguar then won at Le Mans two years in succession, Mike Hawthorn and Ivor Bueb driving the winning car in 1955, and Ron Flockhart and Ninian Sanderson bringing home the Ecurie Ecosse 'D' type ahead of all the works teams at the 1956 Le Mans. Naturally Hodkinson's team were anxious to try the brakes on other chassis, and discs were fitted to the Rubery Owen Maserati with which Peter Collins won the 1955 Silverstone *Daily Express* Trophy Race, and also to Stirling Moss' privately owned Maserati with which he had considerable success when he was not engaged with the Jaguar team. Rodney Clark adopted them for the Connaught Grand Prix team, and Tony Brooks promptly won the 1955 Syracuse Grand Prix, the first Grand Prix victory abroad for a British car since the Sunbeam successes of thirty-one years previously.

Sir William Lyons was watching this continual track-testing

with greatest interest, and as some of the photographs in this book show, he was present on all major occasions when his disc-braked Jaguars were entered. So he agreed with Heynes that discs should be made available on the XK150, and subsequently on the other models. The racing Jags were fitted with a separate servo motor to enable considerably more pressure to be applied to the pads than the thrust of the driver's foot on the brake pedal could normally produce, especially as there were three pairs of pads on each front wheel, and two on each rear.

For road use, however, one set of pads per wheel was found quite adequate, and, although no self-servo action is inherent in disc brakes, it was found that many production cars could dispense with a servo motor without excessive pedal pressure being required. Unlike brakes with drums, which expand as they get hot, the friction material has only to be moved a minute fraction of an inch at each wheel between off and full-power for any one stroke of the pedal. This can therefore be arranged to exert much greater leverage than is considered acceptable with drum-type braking systems.

Tests were carried out on a factory Mk. VII saloon, as well as with XK140 works chassis, and a number of roadworthy advantages of discs soon became apparent. For instance, apart from the fact that there is no fade after repeated heavy applications, there is also no dangerous loss of braking power after the car has gone through water. Apart from the fact that the centrifugal force throws off all water, mud and lining-dust as the discs spin round, the actual contact pressure at the small pads is very much higher than at any part of ordinary shoes, so all foreign matter is automatically squeezed out of the way without affecting braking performance.

Accompanying diagrams clearly show the construction and operation of a disc brake. The assembly shown on page 77 is as used on Jaguar front suspensions. Rear brakes are similar in construction, but are fitted with a mechanically operated handbrake. The disc is attached to the hub, of course, and rotates with the wheel. It is embraced by a caliper which is rigidly fixed to the axle. This caliper carries two hydraulic cylinders each containing a piston and a circular pad of friction material. The cylinders are placed one on each side

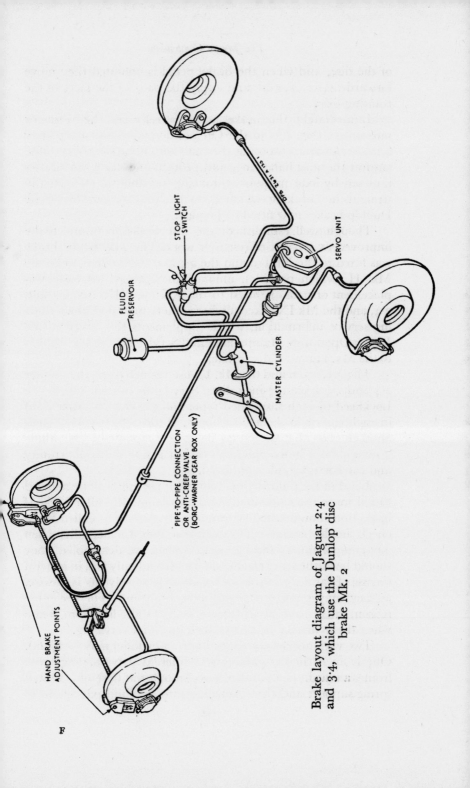

F

STOP LIGHT
SWITCH

DGB 2611 A 125 I

SERVO UNIT

FLUID
RESERVOIR

MASTER CYLINDER

PIPE-TO-PIPE CONNECTION
OR ANTI-CREEP VALVE
(BORG-WARNER GEAR BOX ONLY)

HAND BRAKE
ADJUSTMENT POINTS

Brake layout diagram of Jaguar 2·4
and 3·4, which use the Dunlop disc
brake Mk. 2

of the disc, and when the brake pedal is operated they move forward under pressure and apply the pads to the faces of the rotating disc.

Immediately the brake pedal is released, the retractor pins return the pads to the Off position, which is completely free of the disc. Disposing the pads on either side of the disc ensures thermal balancing, and protects the disc from stresses imposed by axle movement, making possible the consistently straight-line braking which is such a happy feature of the Dunlop brakes now fitted to Jaguars.

Though well established, the disc brakes continue to be improved as a result of research work. The Mk. I-type brake was fitted to the XK150 and the 2·4 and 3·4 models, while the Mk. II (which provides, among other things, for easier replacement of pads) is fitted to the XK150, XK150 S, 2·4 and 3·4, and the Mk IX. Except where otherwise stated, the following service information, which supplements that given in the Jaguar Operating, Maintenance and Service Handbook, applies to the Mk. II type of disc brake.

The XK150 S and the Mk. IX use 12-inch discs, the smaller 2·4 and 3·4 have 11⅜-inch discs. Servo unit in each case is the Lockheed 6⅞-inch suspended type, and the correct brake fluid in each case is Wakefield Crimson. If for any reason overseas another type of fluid has to be used temporarily, the whole system should be completely drained at the first opportunity and the correct fluid substituted.

Level of the fluid in the main reservoir must not be allowed to fall more than one inch (24 mm.) below the filler neck. If inspection shows that very frequent topping-up is called for, a check should be made of the whole system. Incidentally, when any components of the hydraulic system are dissembled, they should be flushed and cleaned in brake fluid only and in general the use of paraffin, petrol or chemical grease solvents is unwise, as they may damage the rubber components. For the same reason, the bench and the hands must be quite free from grease when the hydraulic side is stripped down for servicing.

Two variants of the standard master cylinder may be found. One is an earlier type having a different valve arrangement from standard. The valve passes through the bore of a vented spring support and then protrudes into the fluid passage from the inlet connection. Interposed between the spring support and an integral flange formed on the valve is a small coiled spring. A seal bush carrying an external rubber seal locates between the end of the cylinder body and the underside of the valve flange. The second variant is a master cylinder incorporating an integral reservoir, with a detachable cover secured by bolts, and with the usual type of filler cap. It should be noted that there is a cork gasket between the cover and the reservoir faces.

Many features of the hydraulic system are common, so far as servicing goes, with those of any other type of hydraulically operated braking system. For example, the inclusion of air is indicated by a sluggish response of the brakes, and a spongy action of the pedal. This may be due to air entering at a loose joint, or because the level in the reservoir has been allowed to fall too far. This means bleeding the system completely, as also is the case when any part of the hydraulic system is dismantled.

Before bleeding, clean the whole of the *outside* of the system with petrol so that there will be no chance of dust and grit being worked into any of the components. As with any other system, it is advisable to top up with fresh fluid free from air-bubbles, but if this is not possible then the fluid should be allowed to settle for some hours before being stored again for future use.

To bleed, first check that all connections are tightened, and all bleed screws closed. Fill the reservoir with fluid, then attach the bleeder tube to the bleed screw *on the near-side rear brake*, and immerse the open end of the tube in a small quantity of brake fluid in a small jam-jar. Slacken the bleed screw and operate the brake pedal slowly backwards and forwards through its full stroke. The fluid ejected may show presence of air bubbles, and pumping should be continued until the fluid in the jar is quite reasonably free from bubbles. *Keep the pedal fully depressed* while the bleed screw is closed. The pedal can then be released. This job, as will be seen, necessitates a helper to press the pedal, and to keep it fully depressed on the final stroke until the bleed screw is closed.

Check level in the reservoir before bleeding the off-side rear unit, and repeat this sequence for the other units. It may be necessary to go around all four units again until the whole system is completely free from bubbles. Not until all air is pumped out will the hydraulic system work satisfactorily. Make a final check on fluid level in the reservoir, and then hold down the brake pedal for two or three minutes, with steady pressure, in order to check the system for leaks.

Brake adjustment is automatic during the wearing life of the pads, and these should be checked at frequent intervals. The round friction pads fitted to Dunlop discs have an original thickness of about $\frac{11}{16}$-inch, and when wear has reduced the pads to the minimum permissible thickness of 0·25 inch, the pad assemblies must be removed complete with securing plates. Only the specified Dunlop pad material must be used for replacement.

To fit new pads to the Mk. II brakes, proceed as follows:

1. Remove the nut, washer and bolt securing the keep plate, and withdraw the plate.

2. With a suitable hooked implement engaged in the hole of the lug of the securing plate, withdraw the worn pad assemblies.

3. Thoroughly clean the backing plate, dust seal and the surrounding area of the caliper.

4. With the aid of the special tool (piston re-setting lever, Dunlop Part No. A.O. 103742) press in the piston assemblies to the base of the cylinder bores, as follows.

5. Insert the forked end of the piston re-setting lever into the space between the caliper bridge and one of the piston backing plates, with the fork astride the projecting spigot and its convex face bearing on the piston backing plate. Locate the spigot end of the lever pin in the keep plate bolt hole in the bridge. Pivot the lever about the pin to force the piston to the base of the cylinder. Insert the new friction pad assembly. Repeat this operation for the opposite piston assembly.

6. Replace the keep plate, and secure it with the bolt, washer and nut.

With the earlier Mk. I type of brake, the following procedure should be followed to fit new pads.

1. Disconnect and blank off the supply pipes. Remove the bridge pipes and drain the cylinder blocks.

2. Unscrew the securing bolts and remove the cylinder blocks complete with piston and pad assemblies.

3. Press the carrier plate and cylinder block firmly together to press the piston back into the cylinder, and reset the retractor

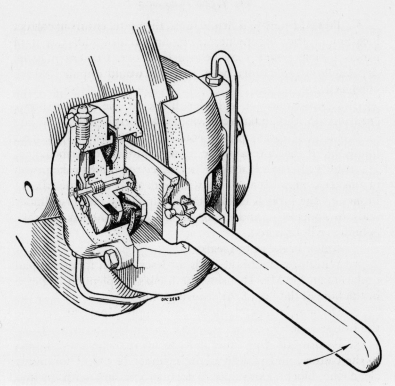

Method of resetting the pistons on the Dunlop Mk. 2 layout, using the special piston resetting lever, Part No. AO. 103742

pins. To do this, press the pin heads into their recesses in the carrier plate, and, holding them in this position, ensure that the retractor bushes are pressed well home into their housings on the outer face of the block.

4. Carefully prise the pad from the carrier plate, using a sharp knife; and clean away any traces of cement from the face of the plate. During this operation be careful not to twist the carrier plate relative to the block, as this may distort the retractor pins. Trichlor-ethylene may be used to clean the carrier plate. This fluid should be used sparingly, and should not be allowed to come into contact with rubber components.

5. Lightly smear the annular face of the carrier plate with Dunlop general-purpose cement. Do not smear the raised centre portion of the plate.

6. Press the new pad firmly on to the plate, ensuring correct location of the alignment screw, and remove all traces of excess cement which may be squeezed out. Cement may be deposited on the caliper bore, and this would impair braking efficiency.

7. Re-assemble the cylinder block to the caliper body, ensuring that the Shakeproof washers are serviceable.

8. Fit the bridge pipes, connect the supply pipes, and finally bleed the system in the manner already described.

At long intervals it may be necessary to renew brake piston or master cylinder seals. This will be described for the Mk. II brakes, as the process is identical so far as the master-cylinder seals are concerned, and minor differences for the Mk. I brake cylinders will be noted.

To renew brake piston seals:

1. Withdraw the brake pads as described in item 2 of pad replacement for Mk. II, using the hooked implement engaged in the hole of the lug of the securing plate.

2. Disconnect and blank off the supply pipe, and remove the bridge pipe.

3. Remove the mounting bolts securing the cylinder blocks to the caliper, and withdraw the cylinder blocks. Thoroughly clean the blocks externally before proceeding with further dismantling.

4. Disengage the dust seal from the groove around the cylinder block face.

5. Connect the cylinder block to a source of fluid supply, and apply pressure to eject the piston assembly.

6. Remove the screws securing the plate to the piston, lift off the plate and piston seal, withdraw the retractor bush from within the piston bore. Carefully cut away and discard the dust seal.

7. Support the backing plate on a bush of sufficient bore diameter to just accommodate the piston. With a suitable tubular distance-piece placed against the end of the piston spigot, and located around the shouldered head, press out the piston fron the backing plate. Care must be taken during this operation to avoid damaging the piston.

8. Engage the collar of the new dust seal with the lip of the backing plate, avoiding harmful stretching.

9. Locate the backing plate on the piston spigot and with the piston suitably supported press the backing plate fully home.

10. Insert the retractor bush into the bore of the piston. Lightly lubricate a new piston seal with brake fluid, and fit it into the piston face. Attach and secure the plate with the screws, and peen-lock the screws.

11. Check that the piston and cylinder bore are thoroughly clean and show no sign of damage. Locate the piston assembly on the end of the retractor pin. With the aid of a hand press, slowly apply an even pressure to the backing plate and press the assembly into the cylinder bore. During this operation ensure the piston assembly is in correct alignment in relation to the cylinder bore, and that the piston seal does not become twisted or trapped as it enters. Engage the outer rim of the dust seal in the groove around the cylinder block face. Ensure that the two support plates are in position.

12. Reassemble the cylinder blocks to the caliper. Fit the bridge pipes, ensuring that they are correctly positioned. (It is absolutely essential that the bridge pipe is fitted *with the near-vertical part of the pipe furthest from the wheel*.) This pipe carries a rubber identification sleeve. Remove the blank from the supply pipe, and connect up.

13. Finally, fit the pad assemblies and the keep plate, and bleed the system as described.

To renew master cylinder seals, the following routine should be followed, both for Mk. I and Mk. II Jaguar types:

1. Ease the dust excluder clear of the head of the master cylinder.

2. With suitable pliers remove the circlip: this will release the push-rod complete with dished washer.

3. Withdraw the piston, and remove the 'O' ring.

4. Withdraw the valve assembly complete with springs and supports. Remove the seal from the end of the valve.

5. Lubricate the new seals with brake fluid, fit the seal to the end of the valve, ensuring that the lip registers in the groove. Fit the 'O' ring in the groove around the piston.

6. Insert the piston into the spring support, ensuring that the head of the valve engages the piston bore.

7. Slide the complete assembly into the cylinder body, taking particular care not to damage or twist the 'O' ring.

8. Position the push-rod and depress the piston sufficiently to allow the dished washer to seat on the shoulder at the head of the cylinder. Fit the circlip and check that it fully engages with the groove.

9. Fill the dust excluder with clean Wakefield No. 3 Rubber Grease.

10. Reseat the dust excluder around the head of the master cylinder.

When any modifications are being made to a Jaguar chassis, as for trials preparation, it is advisable to check at the master cylinder that the brake-pedal linkage provides the requisite free travel of the pedal. Check that when the brake pedal is in the Off position there is no pre-loading of the master cylinder piston, which should abut the inner face of the dished washer at the head of the unit. In the Off position this washer forms the return stop for the brake pedal, and a free axial movement of approximately 0·015–0·02 inches should be felt at the master cylinder push rod.

The Jaguar Operating, Service and Maintenance Handbook gives adequate instructions for adjusting handbrake cable, and reference is made to pad adjustment. It should be noted that the following is a good sequence for handbrake adjustment after renewal of any components, or when adjustment is necessary due to cable stretch, or wear in the linkage.

1. Tighten each handbrake adjuster bolt until the pads 'nip' tightly on the discs.

2. Place the handbrake lever in the fully Off position.

3. Adjust the handbrake cable in accordance with the manufacturers' instructions (e.g. page 34 of the Jaguar XK150 Service Handbook), ensuring that there is no pre-load or slackness in the linkage.

4. Adjust the handbrakes individually. Set the brake clearance by tightening the adjuster bolt until the pads are lightly in contact with the disc, and then slacken the bolt one-third of a turn. This clearance should be reset when the travel of the handbrake lever becomes excessive.

In view of the close relationship between the Jaguar Company and Harry Butler and Harold Hodkinson of the

Dunlop disc-brake unit, it is interesting that similar Jaguar co-operation has been helpful in connection with the development of the Maxaret anti-locking device for road use, and also in the trials of Dunlop tyres for racing and road use.

The Maxaret system was designed by the Aircraft Division of Dunlop, introduced in 1952 as an anti-skid device for aircraft, and is now made under licence in the United States and other countries.

Principle of operation is simple. A small flywheel is rotated by each braked wheel, thus as the road wheel is decelerated, so also is the flywheel. A spring is incorporated in the drive between the road wheel and the flywheel, so that if the rate of deceleration of the road wheel is greater than that which would be experienced during normal braking (that is, if the wheels tend to lock), the spring deflects and allows the relative movement to take place between the flywheel and its drive.

This relative movement actuates a small hydraulic valve to relieve the brake pressure, until the rate of deceleration is reduced and the flywheel is returned by the spring to its normal position relative to the drive. Naturally, if the wheels do not tend to approach the point of locking when the brakes are applied, the rate of deceleration is not sufficient for the inertia of the flywheel to deflect the spring.

Extensive modification of the aircraft Maxaret was needed for road use, and Mr. F. R. Mortimer drew up a confidential report in 1958 showing many of the points—as, for example, the need to reduce size and weight, and the fact that the aircraft type needs a powered hydraulic supply working at about 1,000 p.s.i. This, incidentally, is about the same pressure as there is in pipelines of a Jaguar hydraulic braking system when the pedal is hard down.

Such a powered hydraulic system is already used on the Citroen DS19, but for many reasons it was decided to fit the prototype Maxaret to a Mk. VII Jaguar, and this was given extensive testing on the skid track at Fort Dunlop, on an airfield, and at the Government-sponsored Road Research laboratory.

The test Jaguar was fitted with four entirely separate Maxaret units, with an electrical switching network enabling front, rear, all or none to be used on the skid-pan. As a result of this development work on the Jaguar Mk. VII, much valuable knowledge has been gained, and the weight of the individual Maxaret unit has been reduced to only 2 lb. 5 oz. It is hoped that its first application will be for public-utility vehicles such as police cars, ambulances and fire engines which are occasionally called upon to travel at high speeds and there the risk of a skid-stop is one to be avoided.

Co-operation between Jaguar and the tyre companies has ranged through the years from the great international racing events when 'Lofty' England and 'Dunlop Mac'—under the instructions of Norman Freeman, the senior competitions manager in the tyre field—experimented with every type of tread, cover and tube, under racing and trials conditions, to extensive road tests under normal touring conditions.

Mike Hawthorn, for example, was responsible for much practical testing of Dunlop R.S.4 tyres on his 3·4 Jaguar, especially in the matter of road-holding in the wet, and tyre noise on corners. As a result of such tests in the hands of experienced Jaguar drivers, the Road Speed range was developed, with specially compounded 'cold' rubber to withstand internal heat, great strength of nylon casing, and high resistance to corner squeal.

Tyres of this type are now standard equipment on Jaguar, and the Service manual suggests that every 2,500 miles (4,000 km.) the wheels should be changed over in the familiar 'X' order, that is, front near-side to offside rear, front off-side to nearside rear, or alternatively a '1·2·3·4·5' system bringing the spare into the change-over plan. The sole disadvantage of this scheme, apart from the bother of jacking up every 2,500 miles, is that one is faced with a completely worn set of four or five tyres all at the same time, which presents the ordinary private motorist with a bill for replacement of not inconsiderable proportion. Much can be done, of course, to minimize tyre wear by running at high pressure, bearing in mind that tyre pressures increase with driving-heat.

With the XK150, for instance, Jaguar recommend tyre pressures of 23 p.s.i. (1·6 kg./sq. cm.) front, and 26 p.s.i. (1·85 kg./sq. cm.) rear. With slight loss of comfort the makers agree these pressures can be raised to 30 p.s.i. (2·1 kg./sq. cm.) front and 35 p.s.i. (2·5 kg./sq. cm.) rear when much fast

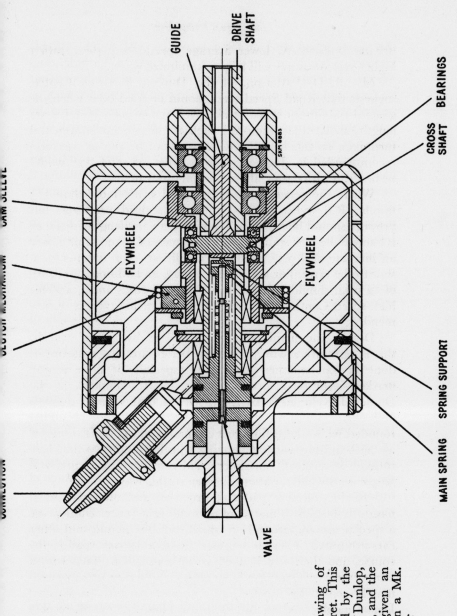

GUIDE

DRIVE SHAFT

BEARINGS

CROSS SHAFT

FLYWHEEL

FLYWHEEL

CAM SLEEVE

CLUTCH MECHANISM

CORRECTOR

VALVE

MAIN SPRING

SPRING SUPPORT

SKM 8885

Cross-sectional drawing of the Dunlop Maxaret. This was first developed by the Aircraft Division of Dunlop, introduced in 1952, and the car version was given an extensive testing on a Mk. VII Jaguar

driving is done. At lower average speeds, too, these rather higher tyre pressures will help to minimize wear.

Mr. P. D. Patterson, of the Dunlop Research Centre, suggests that Road Speed tyres should be used even when the general maximum speed is not over 100 m.p.h., if there are lengthy spells of fast motoring such as one gets on Continental turnpikes. In this case the R.S. tyres can be run at pressures recommended by Jaguar, whereas other types of tyre would be best run with 6 p.s.i. above normal pressure.

Where the general maximum speed is not more than 115 m.p.h., R.S. tyres may be run at standard pressures, but pressure should be raised by 6 p.s.i. where any lengthy distance is likely to be at sustained speeds in excess of 80–90 m.p.h., and an increase of 8 p.s.i. made for conditions even tougher than that to the tyres. For really fast driving, an additional pressure of 12 p.s.i. should be used under those circumstances, and for high-speed Continental work the use of racing tyres is recommended.

Despite the slight bother attached to 'swopping' wheels, this is certainly a wise precaution before any fast motoring is done in bad weather conditions, especially if there is any marked wear on front covers. Mr. W. E. Dunkley, of the Dunlop Development Division, stresses that wear is greatest at the *front* end of the tread block, the leading edge becoming rounded while the trailing edge remains sharp. This is known as 'heel-and-toe' wear. Changing wheel positions so that tyre rotation is reversed can restore skid resistance by as much as 50 per cent when a pattern is worn in this way.

Opinion on tyre patterns, pressures and other factors is naturally not just a matter of personal preference. Dunlop use a special proving ground on which tyres for Jaguar and other cars are tested. There is a 1,300-ft.-long approach road to the course, and there is a banked area about 750 ft. long, with a 1-in-5 transverse banking. The skid-pan area measures approximately 500 ft. by 150 ft., and comprises an area of polished Dorset pebbles, of granite setts supplied by the Liverpool Corporation after 25 years in main roads, and a large area of rock asphalt, lubricated by water when the Jaguar and other tests are made.

Seven

A CAR OF MANY PARTS

SIR WILLIAM LYONS has always been fortunate in his suppliers of components, and he has never been reluctant to admit the part played in Jaguar success by the component and accessory manufacturers.

When he was President of the S.M.M. & T. he defined the place of the suppliers of components by saying: 'While the main decision in producing a new model must rest with the manufacturer, it is not, I think, generally realized how dependent he is upon the co-operation of the major suppliers of components in the industry. The combined resources of these specialist manufacturers and many individual concerns—particularly the large producers of bodies—have manufacturing organizations of a size and efficiency equal to the car manufacturers themselves. . . .'

Approximately half the cost of every British car goes in what are known as 'bought-out' components; the industry in Britain as a whole spends £330,000,000 a year on car components, items ranging from complete bodies and chassis frames, wheels and tyres, to piston rings, door handles, carburetters, plugs, bumpers, nuts and bolts. The Jaguar Company Ltd., in common with every other car-producing firm in Britain, uses components made by the Rubery Owen group. For example, *one in every three* British cars has a Rubery Owen pressed steel axle casing. And the same group provides Jaguar chassis frames.

Rubery Owen are one of the world's largest suppliers of car components, and this huge section of the industry is a credit to a man who rivals Sir William Lyons himself in dynamic leadership—fifty-year-old Alfred George Beech Owen, the head of one of Britain's largest private companies. Its capital is only some £240,000 in £1 ordinary shares. Neverthless, the annual profit from car components and various products including washing machines, kitchen sinks, and power conveyors, runs into hundreds of thousands, and the Owen group turnover averages £25,000,000 a year! Nearly all the shares are owned by the Owen family, and the vast group of more than fifty companies is solely directed by the two Owen brothers, A.G.B. (Alfred) and E.W.B. (Ernest).

Two other brothers, John T. and John W. Rubery began this enormous business 75 years ago when they joined forces to run a small factory in Booth Street, Darlaston, making light steel components. Alfred Owen Sr. joined them in 1893, at the dawn of the 'horseless carriage' era, from which the company made a modest spurt, coming to even greater prosperity when the cycle boom resulted in a demand for steel tubes and fittings.

It was Mr. Owen Sr. who had the vision to see that the clumsy unscientific chassis frames of many cars produced up to the end of the First World War were the cause not only of uneconomic construction, but also resulted in dangerous lack of roadworthiness. He installed powered presses to turn out chassis frames to manufacturers' designs, and in 1929 he was joined by his two sons, Alfred and Ernest. Today the company, which holds stakes in some of the firms for whom they provide components, has expanded into furniture and electrical goods, agricultural and road-making machinery, and they also have manufacturing and subsidiary concerns in Australia and Canada.

This vast family business, on which Jaguar among others depends for essential components, is still run in a paternal way by the Owens. Those who find interest in the private lives of tycoons can discover many points of contrast—and similarity— in the case of Sir William Lyons and Alfred Owen.

Lyons, with his luxurious home, Wappenbury Hall, Leamington Spa, shuns the personal limelight, never preaches, never wastes words, and, as Michael Brown has said, 'takes his place alongside Henry Ford, Lord Nuffield and Sir Herbert Austin—men whose greatness is measured by the distance they have climbed'. Lyons dislikes personal comment, and is credited with retorting to an enquiring Pressman, 'We sell Jaguars, not Lyons.'

Alfred Owen, on the other hand, lives in a small six-bedroomed villa in Sutton Coldfield, run by his wife and a daily help. The key to his love of simplicity is to be found, perhaps, in the fact that he was a Cambridge student, studying for Church of England ordination, when suddenly the death of his father changed the entire course of his life. He assembled the 1,600 workers at the Darlaston factory and told them: 'The organization will be run as a Christian business. Nothing will be permitted which cannot be done with a clear conscience.'

Others in the automobile industry told him he would ruin the business. Far from it. Today this vast group, with its £25,000,000 annual turnover, employs nearly 7,000.

Owen, like Lyons, is a man almost without leisure. And just as Lord Rank spent his Sundays teaching in Sunday school, so Alfred Owen preaches frequently as a lay preacher at mission chapels. Alfred Owen, industrialist and philosopher, directs the business with his brother Ernest and a sister, Mrs. L. Stanley. It is Ernest, an expert engineer, who is in close touch with companies such as Jaguar using the Rubery Owen components.

It must not be supposed, of course, that Jaguar are in any way merely assemblers of their cars; but the position has been reached in industry where even groups such as Rolls-Royce, who used to make their own electrical equipment, now find it better economically to entrust the work of specialist components to specialists. By avoiding unnecessary overheads, Sir William Lyons is able to cost his cars on a more economical basis.

For example, at the present ultra-modern Browns Lane factory the largest presses are 100 tons, which means that only small body items are pressed. Panels are received in batches from Pressed Steel, and these are stored under weather-sheets. On the other hand, Sir William Lyons deemed it necessary to install his own spraying section for the synthetic enamels now used, and the Jaguar factory boasts a £450,000 paint shop, better than most in the industry.

If it were economic or technically advisable for the Jaguar Company to produce, for example, their own body panels instead of leaving this work to specialists, the capital is readily available for the installation of such plant. The Jaguar policy has always been to produce parts as cheaply as possible without any reduction of quality, and often this can only be done by enlisting the aid of specialists outside the Jaguar group.

For example, hypoid axles may come from Salisbury Transmission of Birmingham, the Laycock de Normanville overdrive gear from Laycock Engineering of Sheffield, and propeller shafts from Hardy Spicer of Birmingham—all three companies being members of the automotive division of Birfield Industries Ltd. All Jaguars use Marston radiators, and Marston Excelsior Ltd. is an I.C.I. subsidiary. West Yorkshire Foundries Ltd. provide cylinder heads and other parts; Metal Sections Ltd., of Oldbury, are suppliers of components, as also are L. H. Newton & Co., Ltd. (precision repetition parts, small pressings and 'Sems' assemblies), Intalok, Weathershields (sunshine roof), Richards & Ross Ltd. (tube manufacturers), Charles Stringer Sons & Co., Ltd. (screws) and many more.

No doubt one of the most famous 'components' used on Jaguar cars is the automatic gearbox, a unit in the design of which British engineers have vied with those of Detroit.

Jaguar was among the first British cars to fit automatic transmission as optional equipment, and the Borg-Warner system is now familiar.

Basically the system consists of a hydraulic torque converter and two epicyclic gear-sets in series. This gives three speeds forward, low, intermediate and high, as well as reverse. For the low gear, the three units operate in series, while for the intermediate gear a multi-disc clutch locks up the front epicyclic gear set so that it rotates as a unit. The drive is then through the torque converter and reduction of the rear epicyclic set only. For high gear, a single-plate clutch couples the engine output direct to the gearbox output shaft, thus giving a direct 1–to–1 ratio and bypassing both the torque converter and the gear system.

The mechanical reduction through the box is 2·308 on low gear and 1·435 on intermediate, while the torque converter has an output-input ratio ranging from slightly over 2–to–1 down to 1–to–1. Therefore, there is a perfectly smooth gradation from a maximum reduction of 4·6–to–1 on low gear to a minimum reduction of 1·435 on intermediate. Reverse is obtained without extra gearing. The drive is reversed through the front epicyclic set, and reduced to a ratio of 2·009 × converter, which is 4·34–to–1 in the rear epicyclic set.

The change from intermediate to high is made in a single

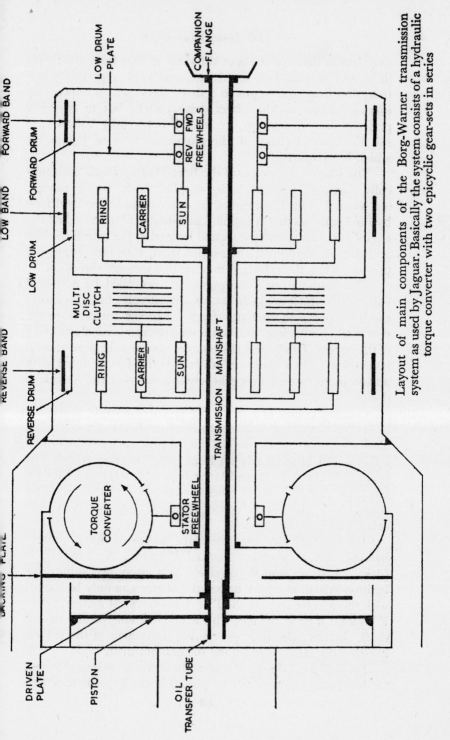

Layout of main components of the Borg-Warner transmission system as used by Jaguar. Basically the system consists of a hydraulic torque converter with two epicyclic gear-sets in series

G

step, but as this step is about the same as that from 3rd to 4th in a conventional four-speed box, and very appreciably less than that from 2nd to 3rd in a three-speed box, it imposes no excessive loads on the direct drive clutch; but to ensure a perfectly smooth pick-up, this clutch is specially 'tailored' to suit the characteristics of the particular type of Jaguar for which it is required.

The whole mechanism of the Borg-Warner box is hydraulically operated, pressure being supplied from two oil pumps, one located at the front end of the gear-box and directly driven by the engine so that it supplies pressure at all times when the engine is running, and the second located at the rear of the box and directly driven off the output shaft, thus only supplying pressure when the vehicle is moving in a forward direction.

The output from these pumps is controlled by a special valve unit, which not only acts as a relief valve but also causes the front pump to discharge freely when the output from the rear pump is sufficient, thus improving the mechanical efficiency of the system. This layout also enables the car to be push-started if necessary—an important advantage the Jaguar fitted with an automatic box has over others with a different and American design.

Controls consist of a manually operated selector valve and a governor-operated valve which controls the gear-changes. The selector valve is coupled direct to a finger-tip-operated lever placed immediately on front of the steering wheel. The position in the XK150 and latest type Mk. VIII and Mk. IX has been changed, as on other models, so that this finger-tip control is at the lower edge of the facia, and not above the column as in earlier models.

The control has five positions, indicated by a pointer moving over a quadrant marked P (park), N (neutral), D (drive), L (low), and R (reverse). As a safety precaution, the ignition system is so wired that the engine can only be started with the selector lever in the P or N positions. Moreover, in the P position a pawl engages with a notched ring on the output shaft, thereby effectively preventing movement of the vehicle in either direction, even on the steepest gradient.

For full availability of engine-braking on a long descent, the lever may conveniently be placed in the L position, at any speed below 40 m.p.h. In this position the transmission will not automatically change out of low gear. It is only in the D position that the governor takes charge, and all gear-changes, up and down, are made automatically in accordance with the combination of vehicle-speed and accelerator-pedal position, increase of speed tending to cause a change up, and reduction of speed tending to cause a change down.

A detent is fitted in the accelerator-pedal linkage, and comes into effect at normal full throttle, but if a special burst of acceleration is required, or speed on a severe gradient, the accelerator pedal can be 'kicked down' past this position to the floor-boards, to effect a change-down to intermediate.

The following figures indicate some of the features of the system on a typical application:

Change from low to intermediate on part throttle at 10 m.p.h., on full throttle at 35 m.p.h.

Change up, intermediate to high, on part throttle at 18 m.p.h., on normal full throttle at 55 m.p.h., and on 'kick-down' at 68 m.p.h.

Change down, high to intermediate, throttle closed, at 12 m.p.h., or higher according to throttle opening. 'Kick-down' may be used for this change at any speeds below 60 m.p.h.

The automatic change-down at 12 m.p.h. disconnects the direct-drive clutch and brings the torque converter into operation, the drag from which at engine tick-over is negligible. It will be seen from the foregoing that in normal driving, apart from the brakes, the whole control is vested in the accelerator pedal. Furthermore, driving convenience is greatly enhanced, and abuse of the car through transmission misuse is entirely avoided.

Another transmission aid which has been given a thorough and satisfactory trial on Jaguar is the Laycock de Normanville overdrive, which was first fitted as optional extra on the Mk. VII, XK140 and the 2·4. Using the overdrive calls for no extra or special knowledge on the part of the driver. There are no additional controls for a driver to cope with, apart from the finger-tip switch which puts the overdrive 'in' or 'out' of operation. There are no worries or extra rules to remember, and using the Laycock overdrive on the Jaguar soon becomes as subconscious a part of driving routine as using a trafficator switch.

The overdrive shows a big advantage at cruising speed. Most drivers' ideas of a reasonable cruising speed differ, but for overdrive motoring it is best described as that effortless speed in top gear when the driver 'feels' the car running well within its power. This is the stage at which the availability of a 'higher-than-top' gear results in quieter, smoother and more economical motoring. Operation of the Jaguar form of the overdrive is simplicity itself. The switch is flicked to the 'in' position, and, without any alteration of the foot controls, an immediately noticeable drop in engine revs—while the car maintains the same road-speed—indicates that the overdrive is in operation.

The Laycock de Normanville system as used on Jaguar comprises an epicyclic gear-train in which planet wheels revolve around the sun wheel and inside the annulus. An ingenious feature is the use of hydraulic operation, whereby the transmission of power passes through the overdrive whether it is in operation or not.

The overdrive passes the engine power to the propeller shaft through a uni-directional roller clutch, the gear-train being inoperative. A sliding splined cone clutch holds the sun wheel and annulus together by means of spring pressure, locking the gear-train solid; and in this way the engine braking is available. This cone clutch also drives the car in reverse. Hydraulic pressure opposes the spring pressure on the splined cone clutch, causing it to engage with the conical brake ring built into the main casing. As the sun wheel and cone clutch are integral, the former is now held stationary, and the annulus is now driven at a higher speed than the gearbox shaft.

Whether engaged or not, the feature of the overdrive is that the driver is able to brake with his engine at all times. A uni-directional roller clutch has its inner member on which are cut inclined surfaces, carried on the drive shaft from the gearbox. The outer member is fitted to the annulus which, in turn, is attached to the propeller shaft, and between the two members is a set of rollers. The roller clutch drives the annulus in one direction only, and in the event of the car over-running the engine, the rollers tend to move down the inclined surfaces

Silverstone, England, 1952. Photograph shows Peter Walker at the wheel of his Jaguar XK120 'C' type in the Production Sports Car Race at Silverstone which was won for the fourth year in succession by Jaguar

Sebring, 1958. Ecurie Ecosse Jaguar at speed

The Tojeiro-Jaguar Mk. IV, one of the several 'Victorious Variants' of the Jaguar. The Tojeiro, designed by Mr. J. M. Tojeiro, has a chassis-frame of the multi-tubular space-frame type, and it is available in complete form with any of the XK variants from the 3- to the 3·8-litre, and with the C- or D-type gearbox

away from the annulus or output member, and so break the drive. This leaves the car without engine resistance to assist braking. The problem is overcome by means of the cone clutch. With overdrive in operation, the engine braking obtains through the stationary sun wheel being prevented from rotation in either direction by the cone clutch.

As fitted to Jaguar the hydraulically controlled epicyclic gear is in a casing mounted directly to an extension at the back of the gearbox, and the control switch on the facia is a simple key marked 'Overdrive—In—Out'. The makers stress that while there is no need to declutch when using the switch, the accelerator should be depressed slightly to get an absolutely smooth change from overdrive top to normal top gear. For normal driving on British roads, the drive is hardly likely to be used effectively at less than 50 m.p.h. on the XK150, but at rather lower limits on, say, the 2·4 and 3·4. Incidentally it should be noted that while Jaguar recommend the main gearbox to be drained at every 10,000 miles (16,000 km.), the overdrive *must* be separately drained, although at first sight the unit may appear to be in common. The large brass drain plug under the unit must be removed when the main box is drained through the orifice at the front of the gearbox.

It is a wise precaution to clean the overdrive oil pump filter each time the box is drained. This is easily accessible through the drain plug orifice, and is secured by a central screw. The filter gauze should be washed in petrol and allowed to dry. Do not clean the gauze mesh with coarse rag. The distance-piece and washers must be replaced with the filter before the central screw is tightened.

It is important to check the gearbox oil level after the car has been run a few miles, following each draining, as a small quantity of oil is retained in the hydraulic system itself, and this naturally brings down the level in the main box. Jaguar recommendations should be followed with regard to gearbox lubricant, and an S.A.E. 30-viscosity lubricant is recommended, for example, for the XK150. With current oils this means Mobiloil A, Castrol XL, Shell X-100/30, Essolube 30, B.P. Energol 30, Duckham's NOL 30, and it is unwise to use any oil of lower viscosity.

With increasing weights of saloon models (the dry weight

of the Jaguar Mk. IX is 35¼ cwt.) there is scope for the application of power steering, and in the autumn of 1958 the new Burman power-assisted steering system became standard equipment on the Mk. IX. Earlier systems applied to other cars, especially those from Detroit, used a normal steering system with a linkage to what is, in effect, a hydraulic jacking system. Burman and Sons have devised a power-assisted system in which the hydraulic system is contained within the steering-box.

The system comprises a hydraulically-assisted recirculatory ball worm and nut-type steering-box, supplied with oil under pressure from an engine-driven pump with a separate reservoir incorporating filters. These parts, connected by flexible hoses, form a self-contained circuit.

With the engine running and steering in the straight-ahead position, the oil flows continuously in an open circuit. Immediately the steering column is rotated from this neutral point, pressure is created in the box, and effort applied to the steering linkage in proportion to that exerted by the driver at the wheel.

Oil from the pump enters the steering-box through the end-cover at the front, and passes through a drilling in the worm shaft. The worm nut is provided with an extension which forms a piston, working in a cast-iron cylinder pressed into the main casing. Hydraulic pressure is applied to the side of the piston appropriate to the direction in which the car is being steered. On the steering-wheel end of the worm-shaft is a co-axial selector valve which controls the admission of oil to the appropriate chamber as it is connected directly to the lower end of the steering column, thus rotary movement of the valve relative to the worm-shaft opens and closes ports, and directs the oil to that side of the piston in operation for the appropriate steering lock.

This movement of the steering wheel causes the valve to open relative to the worm-shaft, by an amount proportional to the steering-wheel effort; it restricts or completely closes the return port in the valve, causing pressure to build up in the operative side of the piston.

When the steering-wheel movement ceases, the valve is centralized by a spring, and by hydraulic pressure in the system

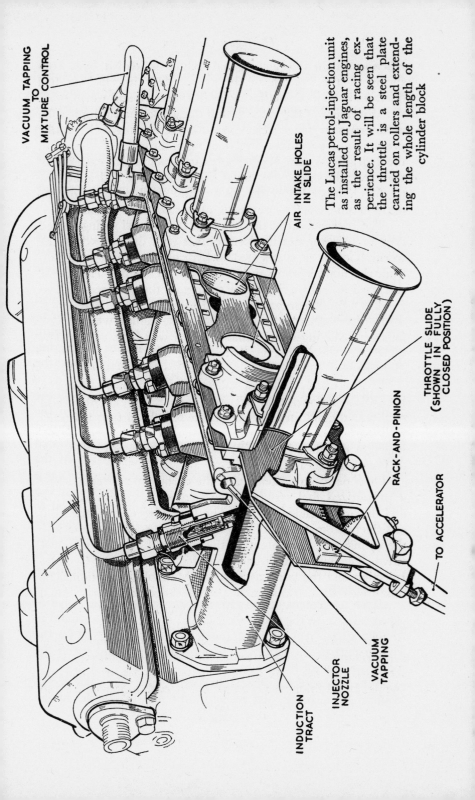

VACUUM TAPPING
TO
MIXTURE CONTROL

AIR INTAKE HOLES IN SLIDE

THROTTLE SLIDE
(SHOWN IN FULLY
CLOSED POSITION)

RACK-AND-PINION

TO ACCELERATOR

INJECTOR NOZZLE

VACUUM TAPPING

INDUCTION TRACT

The Lucas petrol-injection unit as installed on Jaguar engines, as the result of racing experience. It will be seen that the throttle is a steel plate carried on rollers and extending the whole length of the cylinder block reacting on an interlocking ball which is loaded by a coil-spring at the bottom of the valve. This interlocking ball operates in shaped, mating holes in the valve and worm-shaft.

Movement of the valve within the worm-shaft is limited by an interrupted flange which prevents overloading by hydraulic pressure, and permits normal steering in the event of a failure in the hydraulic system. Feed grooves are machined at each side of the valve; the short ones on one side control the hydraulic flow to the chamber below the piston, and the long ones, on the opposite side, the flow to the chamber above the piston.

The rocker-shaft of the box is of the normal spring-loaded type to keep the nut in close contact with the grooves in the worm, but it is supplemented by hydraulic pressure tapped off from the main system; the ball-thrust race at the end of the worm is loaded by a ring of coil springs for the same reason. The result is a small, compact and light-weight unit, entirely separate from any other hydraulic system in the Jaguar, which makes for easier steering when manœuvring a well-laden car at slow speeds, yet which does not detract from accuracy of steering at high speeds.

In an entirely different sphere of development there has been close co-operation between Jaguar and an important section of the industry, and this came to light in 1957 when the record-breaking Jaguar was announced as having petrol-injection designed by the Petrol Injection Development unit of Joseph Lucas Ltd.

On a petrol-injection engine the carburetter is replaced by a pressurized fuel system which meters accurate charges of fuel to each cylinder in turn. The fuel is injected in the form of a finely atomized spray into the intake air, either direct into the cylinder or at a point in the manifold close to the inlet valve. The former is usually referred to as Direct Cylinder Injection and the latter as Port (or Manifold) Injection. The mixture is then compressed and spark-ignited in the usual manner, and the system as used on Jaguar and other cars must not be confused with Diesel-type fuel supply.

The accurate control possible over the amount of fuel supplied to each cylinder under all operating conditions gives increased economy and greater flexibility to a petrol-injection engine. In addition, the removal of the carburetter choke and

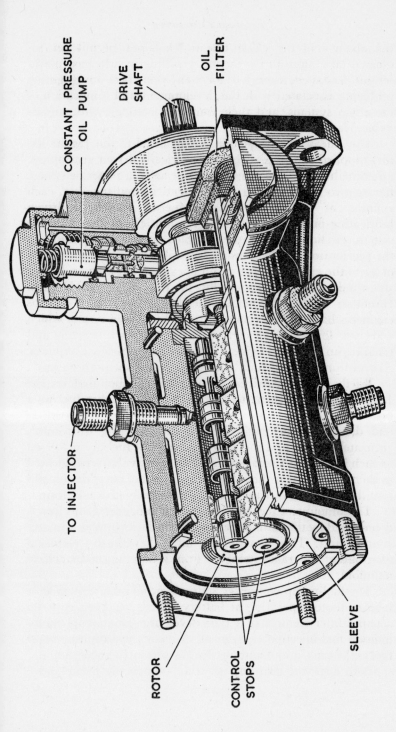

CONSTANT PRESSURE
OIL PUMP

DRIVE
SHAFT

OIL
FILTER

TO INJECTOR

ROTOR

CONTROL
STOPS

SLEEVE

Standard six-cylinder metering distributor as used in the Lucas petrol-injection system

the absence of the exhaust-heated hot-spot permit an increased air charge to the engine, resulting in increased power output. Lucas engineers had for many years been investigating problems associated with the development and application of these fuel systems, and their work was crowned with success at Le Mans in 1957.

The Lucas petrol-injection system fitted to the Jaguar has fuel supplied at 100 p.s.i. by an electrically driven gear pump, and distributed to the cylinders by means of a metering system having two rotating metering elements geared together, each running at one-quarter engine speed. An engine-driven lubricating-pump was provided for lubricating the metering system. A slide-type throttle, coupled by rack-and-pinion to the accelerator pedal, allowed a completely unobstructed flow of air to the cylinders. As a result of extensive testing on Jaguar six-cylinder engines—especially in the hands of Duncan Hamilton and other experienced Jaguar drivers—Lucas engineers have now developed a petrol-injection system which will serve four-, six-, or eight-cylinder engines accurately and reliably, up to 6,000 engine r.p.m., with completely automatic control from cold starting, and through the warm-up stages.

Briefly, a motor-driven primary pump, mounted on the Jaguar chassis adjacent to the fuel-pump, supplies fuel at a pressure of 100 p.s.i. to the metering distributor mounted on and driven by the engine. From the metering distributor, accurately timed and metered quantities of fuel are delivered at each injector in turn; these are of poppet-valve type, located in the manifold near the intake ports, the fuel being discharged into the intake air-stream in the form of finely divided spray.

The amount of fuel metered to the individual injectors is determined by the air charge, and is regulated by the mixture-control unit. This is mounted integral with the metering distributor, and takes its signal from a tapping on the intake manifold.

The fuel-pump comprises a simple gear-pump driven by a built-in motor operating at battery voltage, and incorporates a paper filter element of a type developed for a compression-ignition fuel-injection equipment. A relief valve returns excess fuel to the tank, and maintains the line pressure at 100 p.s.i.

Both engine-driven and electric motor-driven pumps have

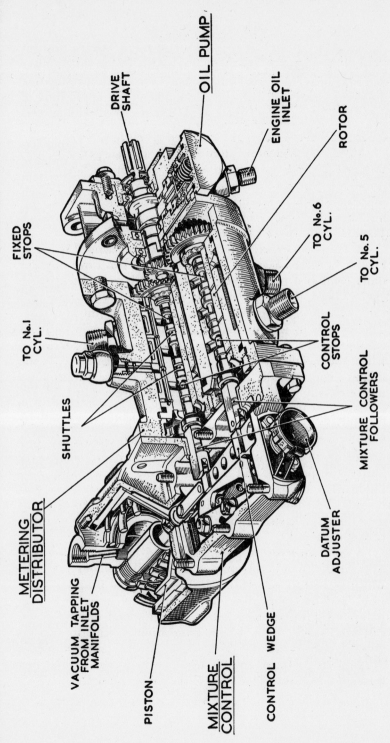

METERING DISTRIBUTOR

VACUUM TAPPING FROM INLET MANIFOLDS

PISTON

MIXTURE CONTROL

CONTROL WEDGE

DATUM ADJUSTER

MIXTURE CONTROL FOLLOWERS

CONTROL STOPS

TO No.5 CYL.

TO No.6 CYL.

ROTOR

ENGINE OIL INLET

OIL PUMP

DRIVE SHAFT

FIXED STOPS

TO No.1 CYL.

SHUTTLES

Six-cylinder-type Lucas metering distributor as developed for the Jaguar XK engine

been developed by Lucas. The latter type has an advantage in that it can be relatively small as a pump, since being independent of the engine there will be adequate flow available for cold-starting under cranking conditions (requiring about 300 per cent excess fuel for reasonably quick starting at 0°F.), and during warm-up, which also required excess fuel.

Most engine-driven pumps need an independent low-pressure feed-pump to maintain the continuous flow of fuel through the pump to scavenge vapour away from the suction side, and this may result in installation complications in some instances. Both types of pump were tried out on a modified Jaguar chassis used for testing fuel-injection.

A six-cylinder metering distributor was developed specially for the Le Mans Jaguars. This consists of two three-cylinder units combined in one rotor, which is driven at one-quarter engine speed, the inlet and outlet ports being so arranged that each cylinder receives one injection of fuel per intake stroke. The shuttles in the two bores are phased to begin injection at intervals of 120 engine degrees. The control stops, by means of which the fuel quantity is adjustable, abut against a face in the mixture control unit. (Improvements in engine performance and economy with the injection system are secured by the extremely accurate control of the fuel feed under widely varying conditions. The automatic mixture control is based on a manifold-depression-operated mechanism, which varies the fuel according to load, with corrections applied for changes in barometric pressure, and for cold-starting and warm-up conditions. This device is attached to the metering distributor, and operates by adjusting the position of the control stops, which determine the length of shuttle stroke, and hence the quantity of fuel delivered.)

A constant-pressure pump, operated by a small eccentric cam on the drive shaft, pumps engine oil at about 105 p.s.i. which is used for preventing leakage of petrol from the rotor ends, and for lubricating the control-stop faces. From the pump, oil is filtered and fed to a longitudinal drilling in the cast-iron sleeve, from which cross-drillings lead to two oil grooves, one at each end of the rotor. At the control-stop end, drillings in the rotor groove lead to the stops, feeding fuel through the centres of the stops to the rubbing faces.

Monza, 1957

Ninian Sanderson on the banking in No. 2 at the 1957 Monza 500-mile race

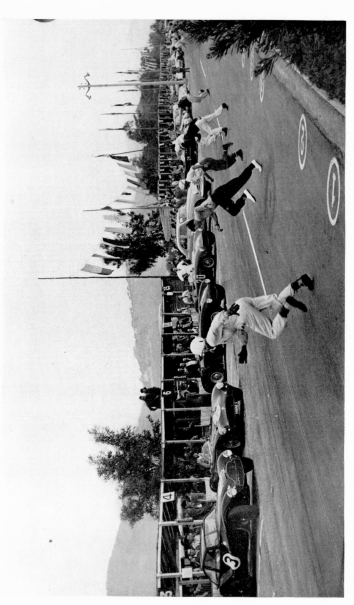

George Abecassis (*second from left, not wearing helmet*) sprints in the Le Mans-type start at the 1954 Twelve Heures d'Hyères

The cast-iron sleeve, complete with rotor and shuttle assembly, is floated in rubber sealing-rings in the aluminium body casting, while between the driving shaft and the rotor driving plate there is a self-aligning coupling which allows for any slight misalignment of the rotor and sleeve assembly on its rubber mounting.

First racing appearance of a D-type Jaguar with fuel injection was at Le Mans in 1955, when a lengthy pit-stop to repair fuel lines (not a fault directly connected with the injection system itself) was a serious handicap, so that the D-type in question finished sixth. Further racing experience was gained later that year in the B.R.D.C.-B.R. & S.C.C. Silverstone event in September 1955. Subsequent road and track tests made by Lucas and Jaguar have put valuable data at the disposal of racing teams such as the Ecurie Ecosse. And when, in the future, fuel-injection systems are used on standard sports and touring cars, this pioneering work on Jaguars will be the basis.

It might indeed prove that this help given to the Jaguar Company by a leading component manufacturer becomes a landmark in technical development of the motor-car engine of the future.

Eight

SERVICING AND SOUPING

THERE is not such a wide range of tuning and 'souping' equipment listed by the component manufacturers for Jaguar as there is available for smaller cars. The XK engine does not lend itself to 'souping' in the same way as Fiat, Ford, M.G. and others, and most Jaguar owners feel that the 210 b.h.p. at 5,500 r.p.m. of the standard 8–to–1 ratio XK engine is quite sufficient for getting from A to B.

There are, however, a number of specialist firms providing off-the-peg tuning equipment which, chosen with care, will certainly help to improve the performance at certain parts of the range, and which may be particularly useful in renovating an older Jaguar or in obtaining greater power output from models such as the 2·4. For maximum performance some Jaguar owners may wish to experiment with different types of carburetters and manifolding, while for all-out performance and increased tractability a low-pressure supercharge may be considered. Naturally, some of the 'souping' methods will involve higher fuel consumption, a greater rate of wear, and probably an increase in noise level. The advice given in this section must not in any way be interpreted as being contrary to the Jaguar Company instructions as explained in the standard Owners' Manuals, and especially where special equipment is fitted to a new car the owner should ensure that the mechanical alterations do not invalidate the guarantee.

Jaguar, in common with nearly all makers today, must limit their responsibility, and the standard six-month guarantee includes the clause: 'The Company accepts no responsibility for any goods which have been altered after leaving the Company's works, or which have been used for motor racing. . . .' Most owners feel that the many years' research and competition experience in the Jaguar engine is enough, and that the fitting of special equipment does not justify possible invalidation. However, for older cars, and for those being converted for special racing or rallying requirements, this may be of little importance.

Jaguar themselves are striving to reduce routine maintenance. With the XK150 and Mk. IX, for example, the minimum greasing interval is 2,500 miles, compared with the 1,000-mile period for many other makes of car. On the XK150, the greasing routine at 2,500 miles is relatively minor, although this is the interval recommended for sump draining, and checking gearbox and axle levels. It is not suggested that the axle and gearbox should be drained and refilled at less frequent intervals than 10,000 miles.

Another fine feature of Jaguar engines, which greatly minimizes servicing, is the longevity of components. I well remember in July 1957, when the Ecurie Ecosse team completed the Le Mans 24-hour race and the Monza 500-mile event, there was no opportunity for 'Wilkie's' mechanics to do more than routine checking of oil filters, ignition settings and plugs. Yet this 3·78-litre high-performance engine completed some 6,000 miles at high speed under gruelling conditions, and the major components of that same engine (e.g. the crankshaft) had also been run at Le Mans, Rheims and Argentina the preceding year.

When the engine was stripped for critical examination, no appreciable wear was found on the crankshaft, there was no loss of tappet clearance on exhausts, no more than 0·004-in. on any of the inlets, bore wear was negligible, the same original 1957 pistons and rings were able to be replaced for another season's racing, and the bearing shells required no replacement, the thin lead overlay being intact.

An equally good standard is maintained by the early $2\frac{1}{2}$-litre and $3\frac{1}{2}$-litre Jaguars of the 1946–48 era which preceded cars with the XK-type engine. Naturally these older cars were less stressed in everyday use, so servicing these cars, which can still be very roadworthy, is generally a matter of overcoming normal wear in engine and transmission as well as making good the ravages of rust after more than ten years. Supplies of spares are still held by some factors, and the following notes for servicing the pre-XK cars should help those without access to the Works manual.

General Maintenance: ($2\frac{1}{2}$-litre). Sump capacity 20 pints, gearbox 2 pints, axle $2\frac{1}{2}$ pints, steering-box $\frac{1}{2}$ pint. S.A.E. 30 oils (modern equivalents Castrol XL, Mobiloil A, Shell X-100 30, Esso Extra 20W/30, Energol 30, Duckham NOL 30) are recommended for engine and gearbox, and S.A.E. 90 hypoid grades (Castrol Hypoy, Mobilube GX 90, Shell Spirax 90 E.P., Esso Expee Compound 90, B.P. Energol E.P. 90 and Duckham's Hypoid 90). With a worn engine where a further limited milage is needed to be covered before a re-bore, a heavier engine oil may be used in summer months (e.g., Castrol XXL, Mobiloil AF, Shell X-100 40, etc), but it is unwise to use a lower-viscosity oil in cold weather, or indeed for any long duration in an attempt to counteract bore wear.

Jaguar advise the oil should be changed at each 3,000-mile interval. Full-flow filter element should be changed at 6,000 miles.

Performance figures. Car in good condition, 45–47 m.p.h. in second, 65–68 in third, and 85–90 m.p.h. in top. Plugs, Champion L.10 (Bosch W145T3, KLG F 20 or TFS 30, Lodge BB14S, A.C. 48, etc.) for the earlier models, and later recommendation Champion N.8. and equivalents. Gaps should be maintained at 0·020–0·025 in. Contact-breaker gap 0·01 in. Tappet clearances, 0·012 in. inlet and 0·015 exhaust, when checked with engine as near running temperature as possible. (Check by turning engine until the valve of which the clearance being checked is fully open; then make one further turn before inserting gap-gauge.)

Top Overhaul

Tightening order for the three rows of cylinder-head nuts is:

	13		7		2		4		10		16		
19		12		6		1		9		15		18	
	14		8		5		3		11		17		

When grinding-in valves seating angle is 30 degrees for inlets and exhausts. Note that each rocker arm has a solder-sealed orifice containing a felt wick. After extensive milage it

George Abecassis, of the HMW-Jaguar team, driving the famous 1954 car, XPE2, at the B.A.R.C. 21st Members' Meeting at Goodwood, 17th March 1956

Copyright: Charles Dunn

Le Mans, France, 1951. Photograph shows Stirling Moss at the wheel of his Jaguar XK120 'C' with which he obtained a record lap of 105 m.p.h.

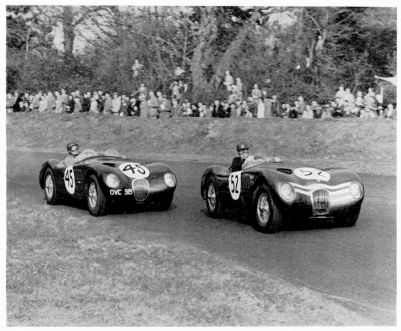

Tony Rolt (car No. 52) leading J. Duncan Hamilton at one important moment of the 1954 British Empire Trophy

The Lyons Trophy, 1951, won by J. Duncan Hamilton in his own specially prepared XK120

is a good thing to replace these wicks and seal afresh with solder. New rubber distance pads on the engine-mounting studs should also be fitted if, during a major overhaul, the engine is lifted out of the frame.

About 0·006 in. bore wear is permissible before a re-bore is necessary, and piston clearances in the bores should not exceed approximately 0·0035 in. Oversize pistons in groups up to 0·04 in. are available, and beyond that limit the block will need to be sleeved. Gudgeon-pin diameter is 0·75 in. Wear on journals and crankpins should not exceed 0·003 in. A new or reconditioned oil-pump should be fitted if there is excessive gear wear. Check the gap between gear face and the cover. This end clearance should not exceed 0·006 in. Check right at the outer tip end of the teeth for clearance from the cover.

Incidental note. As the Jaguar mascot can be purchased separately as a spare part, some owners of older models are tempted to fit them to the radiator cap. The 7-inch-long mascot is set well back on the bonnet of an XK-type Jaguar, but the projecting figure can constitute a danger on earlier cars, and this has in fact been the subject of a police prosecution, when the court held that the fitting of a mascot in a non-standard position can be a source of danger.

XK-Type Engines
Tuning

Plugs. With earlier-type XK engines as fitted to the XK120 and Mk. VII, Champion L.10S was recommended for the 7-to-1 ratio unit, and Champion N.A.8 for the 8-to-1 ratio engine, and both types should be gapped to 0·022 in. (0·56 mm.) With the range of plugs recommended by Jaguar for the XK150 the correct gap is a fraction wider, precisely 0·025 in. (0·64 mm.) With the first specifications of distributor fitted to the XK engine (XK120, etc), the makers advised a contact-breaker gap of 0·012 in, but with the later engines a wider gap of 0·014–0·016 in. (approximately 0·36–0·41 mm.) is advised.

Lowered contact-breaker spring tension can sometimes cause misfiring at speed, and other symptoms of ignition trouble. Correct spring tension, measured at the points, is approximately 22 oz.

Valve Clearances. It is most important when checking tappet clearances on a dismantled head that each camshaft should be fitted individually, and one line of valves checked before the other camshaft is then fitted. If one camshaft be rotated with the other in place, and some valves partly depressed, damage may result from inlet and exhaust valves fouling.

Correct clearances with the later XK150-type engine are: inlet, 0·004 in.; exhaust, 0·006 in. Tappet adjusting pads are available in steps of 0·001 in., in a range etched with an indicating letter A to Z. These same clearances are also correct for the XK engine as fitted to the Mk. VII, but the makers recommended a slightly wider gap-setting for the XK120, namely 0·006 in. inlet and 0·008 in. exhaust.

If it is necessary to fit new tappet guides to earlier engines on which there is noticeable wear, replacement guides (Jaguar Part No. C.7262) can be obtained. The old guide must be bored out (taking great care not to damage the cylinder head by boring unnecessarily wide, beyond the point when the old guide collapses). When fitting the new guides, the head can simply be heated in an oven from cold to about 450°F.

Carburetters. With late-type XK150 engines, after any major overhaul and before attempting any tuning, the contact-breaker, tappet and plug gaps must be set as described. Ignition timing of the standard 8-to-1 engine is 6 deg. B.T.D.C. When the owner is satisfied that these settings are correct, distributor-advance settings should be varied before any new carburetter settings are attempted, as the carburetter performance will be impaired if there is too extreme a degree of advance or retard. The makers suggest that not more than six 'clicks' of the micrometer adjustment should be attempted, and the effect of this should be verified by road performance.

Before checking carburetter tuning it is advisable to remove air pipe and cleaner. Mixture strength of both carburetters must be identical as a basis for any further tuning. To start, put jets in their highest positions (screw in the mixture-adjusting screws), and verify visually if necessary by removing the suction chamber and piston. Give an additional $3\frac{1}{2}$ turns to the mixture screws after they have been screwed in to a position when the jets begin to move.

It is advisable to check that both throttles are synchronized.

This is done by slackening one of the clamp bolts on the short coupling shaft and checking that both butterflies are completely closed at the identical position. Then tighten clamp bolt.

A good plan used by Ecurie Ecosse and other mechanics to ensure synchronization is the use of the 'sucking' test. When the engine has been warmed up and is firing evenly, take a short length of rubber garden hose, place one end to the ear as a sort of stethoscope, and then insert the other end in turn into each carburetter intake. It will soon be detected if, at tick-over speed of 500–600 r.p.m., each carburetter is 'sucking' to the same degree as the other. This check by ear is surprisingly accurate. If any alteration of setting is needed to get equal 'suck', simply rotate one of the two volume screws.

Mixture strength of the individual carburetters can then be checked, starting with the front carburetter. With the blade of a long screwdriver, lift the piston by about 1/32–1/16th in. If there is no detectable change of engine speed, this indicates the mixture strength is correct. A weak mixture is indicated by an immediate slight drop in tick-over speed, while if the mixture is on the rich side, the engine speed will increase slightly as the piston of the front carburetter is raised. Alter the mixture-adjusting screw until there is no noticeable change of engine speed, and then repeat the test on the rear carburetter in the same way. The mixture-adjusting screws are screwed in (clockwise) to weaken the mixture. It may be necessary to reset the slow-running screws after any wide variation is made of mixture strength, and care must be taken that the slow-running volume screws (these alone govern idling speed) are given a well-balanced adjustment on both carburetters.

On older engines where there has been some wear, it may be necessary to replace carburetter needles. Standard needle for the Mk. VII was SM, and RF for the XK120. For extra economy a weak mixture results from the use of an SK needle in the Mk. VII engine, and RG in the XK120. Metal polish must not be used when the dashpot is refitted, as polishing the spindle may upset correct functioning of the needle and mixture control. The top of the hollow piston chamber must be kept filled with engine oil, and, if this dries out and is not checked at every 2,500–5,000 miles, a sluggish dashpot will cause a weak mixture and resulting poor acceleration.

Wear in the needle-valve of the float chamber may cause an alteration in float-chamber fuel level, and consequent level of fuel at 'static position' at the jets.

To correct this, remove each float-chamber cover, and place a ½-inch round bar across the rim of the flange-fitting of the cover, and under the lever and spigot. In this position the needle-valve should just be closed, and the ½-inch bar should slide freely under the slightly curved tongues of the lever. If it does not, gently bend the lever *after* the forked lever has been removed. If any attempt is made to bend it while in position, the point of the needle-valve may be damaged.

Some checking of the starting carburetter may be necessary on older engines. Surrounding the primer valve is a large hexagon nut which when turned clockwise weakens the mixture. If there is occasional difficulty in cold-starting, and the engine fails to run regularly until eventually warmed up, enrich the mixture by turning the nut anti-clockwise until the engine runs without any trace of lumpiness or hunting. Incidentally, although the H.6 carburetters are fitted to 120 and Mk. VII engines, there are minor differences in earlier models. On later engines the starting carburetter is a separate unit, while on earlier engines it is an integral part of the rear carburetter float chamber. The starting carburetter should cut out at 35°C.

Overhauling

Sequence for slackening and tightening cylinder-head nuts is as follows (camshaft drive right):

						15	17
15	7	5	1	3	9	11	19
14	10	4	2	6	8	12	20
						16	18

Valve-seat angle is 30 degrees, inlet, and 45 degrees, exhaust. When tightening cylinder-head nuts it should be noted that the recommended torque is 650 lb. ins.

To simplify a major overhaul of an older-type engine, it should be noted that a number of components and units can be supplied factory-reconditioned on an exchange basis.

Such items as connecting-rods, crankshaft, clutch and clutch plates, oil- and fuel-pumps, water-pumps and thermostats can be obtained, in addition of course to the electrical units available under the well-known Lucas exchange scheme which covers Jaguar dynamos, distributors, starter-motors and other accessories.

Cylinder-block material is chrome iron, and while the nominal bore is 83 mm. (precisely 3·267 in.) the maximum re-bore size advised by Jaguar is 0·76 mm. (0·03 in.) If liners are to be fitted in an old-type engine, correct bore size should be approximately 3·392 in. If connecting-rods need to be replaced owing to excessive wear of big-end (steel-backed shell-type, white metal) or little-end (steel-backed, phosphor-bronze), it should be noted that the connecting-rod end clearance should not exceed 0·009 in. When tightening down connecting-rod bolts, do not exceed 450 lb. ins. torque.

Replace the oil-pump under the factory exchange scheme if there is excessive wear, as oil pressure (hot) in the older-type engine should be a steady 40 lb. at 2,000 r.p.m. When measuring clearance between the body face and gear face, there should not be more than 0·007 in. gap. This can easily be tested with a straight-edge placed across the faces. End-clearance should also be checked, from tooth to body-side, and this must not exceed 0·004 in.

With all these engines there is a suffix '7' or '8' after the engine number denoting the compression ratio. Either Brico or Aerolite pistons may be found in either flat-crown (7–to–1) or domed-crown types. Each make of piston (of identical type) is interchangeable, but they must be properly matched and there should be no difference exceeding 3·5 grammes. They are available, in both makes, in a number of oversizes including 0·005 in., 0·01 in., 0·015 in., 0·02 in. and 0·03 in.

When checking bearing measurements in the process of overhauling an older XK120 or XK140 unit, use may be made of the Plastigauge precision bearing measurer. Kits are supplied by the Plastigauge Manufacturing Co., 181 Brighton Road, Croydon, Surrey. The kit comprises a supply of wax-like Plastigauge rod 0·025 in. in diameter, and a carefully calibrated scale. With this measurements may be taken directly showing the clearance of any split-type bearing. When a portion of the plastic rod is clamped in the bearing, it is flattened to a degree depending on the clearance, and by using the scale the clearance can immediately be read off.

For specialist tuning of older engines it is very advisable to work directly from the Service Manual, as much of the advice given in this section is the result of practical experience by owners and servicing mechanics of outside organizations, and may or may not tally with official Jaguar recommendations.

If tuning is being done and a complete overhaul is contemplated to increase output, advantage may be taken of the special Iskenderian American-made competition camshafts available in kit form for the Jaguar engine. Iskenderian have produced a technical booklet *Valve Timing for Maximum Output* which can be obtained, as can the camshafts, on order from Motor Books, 41–42 Parliament Street, London S.W.1. Customers' cams can be accepted for credit by Iskenderian provided they are within certain set limits.

Miscellaneous

When checking compression pressures on a worn engine, note that pressure may vary according to oil viscosity and engine temperature. Jaguar advise that the test should be made at running temperature (70°C), when the pressure achieved with the XK120 7–to–1 ratio engine should be 105 p.s.i., and 120 p.s.i. for the 8–to–1 ratio engine.

Noise may be caused if the revolution-counter and speedometer drives are not properly lubricated, and it is a mistake to attempt to correct a 'ticking' drive by the use of stiff grease or wax. The flexible shaft should be withdrawn, cleaned and smeared with a thin graphited grease. Then return the shaft, wipe off excess at the casing ferrule.

It is important to change the engine oil filter element every 5,000 miles. There is a bypass valve fitted in the filter assembly, and when the element is completely blocked by oil contaminations this bypass comes into operation, with the result that the pressure as indicated on the gauge drops by some 5–10 lb. Before inserting the new element, carefully wash out the inside of the filter body with a petrol-dipped cotton rag free from fluff, allow to dry, and take care that the rubber seal in the head of the filter is well in place.

Jaguar advocate the use of an upper-cylinder lubricant, and for the later-type engines specify Mobil Upperlube, Castrollo, Shell UCL or Donax U., Esso UCL and Adcoid Liquid. Advantage may also be taken of a graphited upper-cylinder lubricant such as that blended by T. R. Parry & Co., Ltd., Castor Street Oil Works, West India Dock Road, London, E.14. This company, the producers of Penrus oil widely used by many specialist competition and servicing teams, also market a colloidal graphited oil which can be used generally, and which has special advantages in obtaining a wear-resistant surface to bearings and bores after an engine overhaul. It should be noted that while graphited oils are not specially a Jaguar recommendation, they are technically satisfactory with the oilways and filter of the XK engine.

Molybdenum disulphide is also widely used as an oil additive (although not specially on the recommended Jaguar list), and, like colloidal graphite, is an unexcelled lubricant. Many makes of both type of additive are on the market. The experience of certain Jaguar racing and competition teams is that 'molysulphide' will probably stand up to high temperatures and stresses a little better than graphite, and for racing it has some advantage. For high-speed touring and under normal running its chief disadvantage is its greater cost. Moreover, in an engine not used regularly, or perhaps used only occasionally at maximum output, there is a tendency for molysulphide to 'settle out'. It is twice as dense as graphite, so that there is an obvious possibility that it will settle out of the engine oil quicker than graphite unless it is adequately stabilized. An acid element tends to form in any crankcase, and it should be noted that whereas molysulphide can be dissolved in a strong concentration of acid, graphite cannot be dissolved.

When a Jaguar engine is stripped for a major overhaul, the opportunity can be taken to have the crankshaft and flywheel assembly balanced. A quotation can be obtained for this, as well as for re-sleeving and boring, and re-grinding crankshafts, from Laystall Engineering Co., Ltd., 53 Great Suffolk Street, S.E.1. This company has done much mechanical work for the Ecurie Ecosse cars.

It may be considered worth while modifying the existing heads of 2·4, 3·4 and 150-type engines, and this work can be undertaken by Barwell Motors Ltd., Leatherhead Road, Chessington, Surrey.

With the 2·4 engine, the cylinder-head modification is as follows: enlarged, re-shaped and polished inlet and exhaust ports. Enlarged and radiused inlet valve throats. Reduced valve seats. Combustion chambers polished. Inlet valves modified. Induction manifold modified and polished to match ports. All valves ground-in and head built up complete with crankshafts. Modified carburetter setting to suit increased gas flow which is obtained from this modification.

The following figures show the improvement resulting from these modifications, which take about five days and cost approximately £34, with £15 extra for work on car, including tuning and gaskets.

R.P.M.	Stock 2·4	Modified Engine
1,000–2,000	7·0 seconds	6·2 seconds
1,500–2,500	7·3	6·3
2,000–3,000	7·3	6·4
2,500–3,500	8·6	7·5
3,000–4,000	9·7	8·5
3,500–4,500	12·9	11·0
4,000–5,000	16·9	13·6

Similar modifications can be made for the 3·4 engine. It is not quite such a straightforward matter obtaining 'souped' performance with the XK120, XK140 and variants, as of course the design is admitted, even by the specialist tuners, to be one of the most efficient in production today. Therefore improvements can only be made by careful modification and tuning. The Barwell modification on the XK120 has a specification as follows: Enlarged, re-shaped and polished inlet and exhaust ports. Enlarged and radiused inlet valve throats. Reduced valve seats. Combustion chambers polished. Inlet valves modified. Induction manifold modified and polished to match ports. All valves ground-in, and head built up complete with camshafts. This work also takes five days, and costs approximately £36, plus extra for carriage, tuning, gaskets, etc.

A top-gear acceleration test of an XK120 after Barwell modification gave the following figures, with overall maximum speed of the particular car raised from 102 m.p.h. to 115 m.p.h.:

M.P.H.	Stock XK120	Modified XK120
20–40	5·2 seconds	5·0 seconds
30–50	6·0	5·2
40–60	6·8	5·4
50–70	7·8	6·0
60–80	8·8	7·6
70–90	11·4	8·4
80–100	14·4	10·0

An XK140, following similar Barwell modification, was found to show a top-gear acceleration improvement of corresponding scale to the foregoing, 60–80 m.p.h. being reached in 5·9 seconds compared with 7·2 seconds on the car before modification.

On the 2·4 model, twin Solex is current equipment, while twin S.U.s are used on other models. The Type B.32 PBI-5 carburetter is used, and a technical brochure on this can be obtained direct from any Solex stockist. Twin Solex 35 HBFD carburetters can be used to modify and modernize the 1938–1951 3½-litre Mk. V.

It should be noted that there are two types of Solex specification for the 2·4, depending upon the compression ratio, and the following table shows variations for the 7–to–1 and 8–to–1 ratios, with suitable jet, choke and other details for the B.32 PBI-5 carburetter.

Correct Setting	7–to–1	8–to–1
Choke tube	23	24
Main jet	110	110
Correction jet	200	180
Pilot jet	50	
Pilot air bleed	120	
Emulsion tube	14	
Pump jet	55	
Economy jet	—	
Starter jet (petrol)	105	
Starter jet (air)	4·5	
Float	5·7 gr.	
Needle valve	15	
Pump type	72	

Among the low-pressure superchargers available for Jaguar are the Arnott and the Shorrocks.

The belt-driven Arnott supercharger, produced by Carburettors Limited, Grange Road, London, N.W.10, can be readily fitted to XK and Mk. VII and VIII.

'Supercharging' is in itself a misleading term when applied to low-pressure boost, and the expression 'capacity filler' might be more accurate. Normally the mixture in the carburetter at atmospheric pressure flows into the vacuum created in the cylinders by the suction stroke of the pistons. The volume thus admitted may obviously not be the full capacity of the cylinders at atmospheric pressure, and consequently the full efficiency of the engine is not obtained. The advantage of supplying the mixture to the cylinders under a moderate boost, instead of the pistons having to absorb power in sucking in the mixture, is obvious, and the power developed from a fully charged cylinder is as much as a third greater than normal. In addition to the greater power available from an engine when 'fully charged', the power curve continues to rise with the engine speed far beyond the point at which the normal engine begins to fall off in performance. It is also claimed by the makers of supercharging accessories that the more even distribution of the gas when under pressure definitely enables a supercharged engine to use less petrol for a given b.h.p. output.

The Arnott supercharger can be fitted without too much extensive modification to the XK120 or Mk. VII under-bonnet arrangements, and the standard 500 JSH unit can be used.

A standard Shorrock supercharger cannot be supplied for Jaguar, owing to restricted under-bonnet space, but modifications may be made by private owners to blowers for other engines. For example, the M.G. driven by the late 'Goldie' Gardner in May 1939 at Dessau, Germany, was the first car in the world, in Class G, to exceed 200 m.p.h. Fitted with a Shorrock supercharger developed from a standard unit, the M.G. Special driven by Stirling Moss at Utah broke five international Class F records, including the flying kilometre at 245·64 m.p.h. Details of these units can be obtained from Shorrock Superchargers Ltd., Church Street, Wednesbury, Staffs., a company which is one of the Owen group which also supplies Jaguar chassis frames.

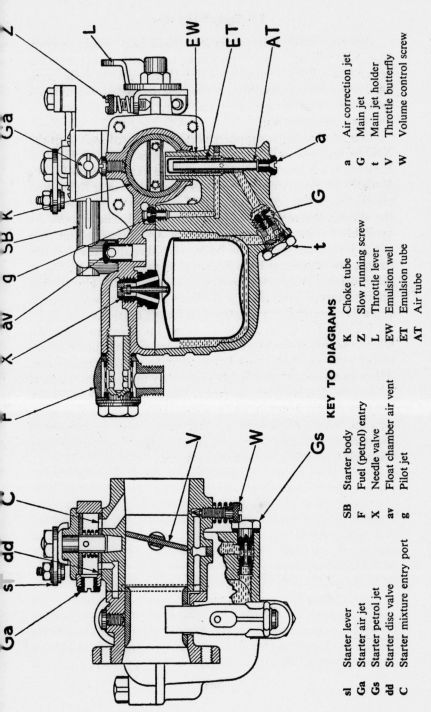

KEY TO DIAGRAMS

sl	Starter lever	SB	Starter body
Ga	Starter air jet	F	Fuel (petrol) entry
Gs	Starter petrol jet	X	Needle valve
dd	Starter disc valve	av	Float chamber air vent
C	Starter mixture entry port	g	Pilot jet

K	Choke tube	a	Air correction jet
Z	Slow running screw	G	Main jet
L	Throttle lever	t	Main jet holder
EW	Emulsion well	V	Throttle butterfly
ET	Emulsion tube	W	Volume control screw
AT	Air tube		

Assembly of the Solex HBF type. This shows the general construction of the 35 HBFD, which is the current Solex conversion for the 1938–9 and 1946–9 1½-litre Jaguar

After mechanical improvements have been made to early type XK120's and 140's, the owner may wish to get a rather better standard of weather-proofing than is given by the standard hood of the sports tourer. Possibly the easiest way of renovating and improving a car in this direction is by the fitting of a detachable hard-top.

One of the biggest suppliers of stock-size hard-tops to fit the XK120 and 140 is Universal Laminations Ltd., 58 Holland Park Mews, London, W.11. The standard hard-top with P.V.C. Vynide outer covering, normal window and quarter lights, and plastic headlining, costs £70, and £19 10s. extra is charged for the sliding Perspex sidescreens. Wrap-round windscreens are available at an additional charge of £5. These saloon tops weigh just under 30 lb. The basic glass-fibre shell is extremely strong, and a top has been known to support the weight of an XK120 when completely overturned in a crash. The shell is approximately $\frac{1}{8}$-in. thick, and allows maximum headroom as it needs no supporting construction on the outside.

Inch-deep recesses are made round the door openings into which the side-screens or winding windows close, and these are sealed with soft draught-excluders to make a weatherproof seal. The tops are seated on soft felt where they meet the car surface.

On the XK120 and 140 two separate fittings are necessary to allow for variations in body measurement. On the first occasion the bare glass-fibre shell is trimmed to the exact shape of the cockpit and windscreen. Then a second fitting is made after the shell has been trimmed and covered.

Nine

BUYING A USED JAGUAR

A JAGUAR, generally, is a very safe car to buy secondhand, as spares are readily available, the service from the factory, from main distributors and specialist concerns is very reliable, and the design is straightforward.

On the other hand, most models except the early 1½-litre cars have large six-cylinder engines necessitating a definite level of maintenance and upkeep, and it is important to ascertain as closely as possible what sort of servicing has been given to the car before it was put on the used-car market.

Jaguars six and seven years old may be a good proposition if well serviced in the past, as they will be at the minimum point of their depreciation scale. But it should be kept in mind that a Jaguar is a 'social landmark' to a certain type of owner, who may find in course of time that he has no margin left after facing petrol, insurance and other bills which are bound to be heavier than with a 10- or 12-h.p. car. The result may be that greater deterioration sets in, and so whether a purchaser can expect to find a really mechanically clean car or not really depends upon the assessment of the former owner as much as of the car itself.

Such items as frequent oil changing, use of the correct (and not inexpensive) oil in a Jaguar fitted with automatic transmission, use of the correct brake fluid, spraying the chassis with a rubberized, zinc-bearing or other anti-rust compound: these and many other maintenance points are really a matter of money, and of how much or little the owner likes to spend on his car. When vetting a used car it is naturally not always a simple matter to discover if correct maintenance schedules have been adhered to, and this should be the first task for any potential buyer.

Reputable dealers are nearly always willing to produce the car's registration book on demand to potential customers; and although of course it may not be possible to obtain the name and address of the former owner, and to contact him to check details, examination of the registration details can disclose much, such as the regularity with which the car has been taxed.

The casual non-trade buyer examines the classified columns of *The Motor* and *The Autocar*, and the 'Cars for Sale' columns of his local paper. The advertising pages of *Motor Sport*, *Autosport* and similar journals are useful for older Jaguar XK120's and XK140's, and for specialist racing C- and D-types. But it must be realized that the prices quoted in all such advertisements are not a trade value. They are merely an indication of price *asked*, which may well be 15 per cent or more above prices actually paid in completed deals.

For years the motor trade has been accustomed to two tables of prices, *Glass's Guide* (available for the trade only, and usually jocularly known by Jaguar dealers and others as 'The Little Black Book'), and the *Measham Magazine*, published monthly at 2s. 6d. by Measham Publications Ltd. In addition, *The Garage and Motor Agent* supplies a fortnightly used-car market report to its readers.

It is impossible to quote actual figures for current second-hand Jaguars, as the general view is that prices a month old are already stale, and that quotations on almost any car more than six or eight weeks old can be very misleading. There are several factors why a car of the class of a Jaguar may show considerable variation in secondhand value. Where one is concerned with the purchase of a car costing £1,000 or more secondhand, and consuming perhaps 20–25 m.p.g., then a number of current factors can quickly affect local values. A petrol shortage, or the threat of rationing, an unexpected change in petrol tax, or new legislation affecting credit facilities or parking restrictions—all these things and more can affect a comparatively expensive used car, occupying some fifteen feet of road-space.

However, as price is naturally one of the first factors to be taken into consideration in purchasing a used car, it is necessary to consider the depreciation factor on various Jaguar models, and we can take prices in the summer of 1959 as a basis. By this period the fears of petrol rationing, as at the time of the Suez crisis, had subsided, and the various Income Tax and Purchase Tax concessions made a slight turn in favour of the larger, more luxurious and faster car. It is therefore a stable period for comparison.

Measham quotations are a good basis, because the month-by-month lists are available to the public and the figures given here can be modified at any future date in accordance with a general trend of depreciation. It should be noted that there are three classes of prices given in these quotations.

Class 1 is with cars where the bodywork and interior are in first-class condition. Brakes, chassis, engine, transmission and all mechanical parts are in good order, not requiring attention. All tools, accessories and standard equipment as supplied by Jaguar to be with the vehicle. Cars in this class will have done a relatively low milage, averaging about 9,000 miles annually, and will have received a high standard of maintenance.

Class 2 is the 'Measham Average Condition', and is as follows: *Bodywork*: Paintwork reasonable for age of vehicle and comparatively free from corrosion. There should be no evidence of major accident damage, and the upholstery should be free from holes and tears. *Chassis*: Free from cracks, repairs, welds and plating. There should be no distortion or loose rivets. *Engine*: Cylinder blocks to be free from cracks and welds, and should not have any oil or water leaks. The engine should maintain normal oil pressure and should not require a re-bore. *Gearbox*: Reasonably quiet on all gears, and all gears capable of staying in under all driving conditions. *Clutch*: Quiet in operation, not slipping, and no excessive judder on take-off. *Rear Axle*: No undue noise, normal play between crown wheel and pinion, and no oil leaks. *Suspension*: All types of suspension to be correctly set up and (where applicable) no oil leaks. Road springs should have no broken leaves, and there should be no excessive wear in the shackles. *Steering*: Steering-box should have normal free movement, no excessive wear in joints or king-pins, or bushes. There should be no tendency to wander or wobble at any road speed. *Brakes*: Hand and footbrakes should be in serviceable condition. Operation should be even, and no immediate attention necessary. *Tyres*: Free from cuts and side-wall weaknesses. Should have at least 2–3,000 miles of safe usage. *Electrical*: Starter and dynamo functioning normally and all essential accessories working correctly. Wiring harness in reasonable condition. Battery should be able to retain a charge. *Equipment*: Starting handle, jack (where applicable), wheelbrace and spare wheel at least to be with the vehicle. Small tools may be expected on a car which is no more than two or three years old.

These details are listed so that fair comparison may be made with the Measham figures quoted for recent Jaguar models; also this is a guide when vetting used Jaguars, as this list gives the major points to check.

The Measham Class 3 includes vehicles which fall short of the standards set in Class 2, and consist primarily of those which have done a high milage, or which have been neglected from a mechanical point of view. One or more major defects may be expected, but it should be possible for the vehicles to be restored to average condition.

On this basis, the following is a fair average of Measham quotations up to the spring of 1959, and these figures will serve as a basis for future transactions, allowing for continuing depreciation.

Model	Year	Measham Quotations in £		
		Class 1	Class 2	Class 3
2½-litre saloon	1949	240	215	170
Mk. V saloon	1949	280	250	200
	1950	320	290	230
	1951	365	330	265
Mk. V d.h. coupé	1949	295	265	210
	1950	340	305	245
	1951	385	345	275
3½-litre saloon	1949	230	205	165
Mk. V 3½-litre saloon	1949	275	245	195
Mk. V 3½-litre d.h. coupé	1949	290	260	210
	1950	330	295	235
	1951	380	340	270
Mk. VII saloon	1950	365	330	265
	1951	400	360	290
	1952	445	400	320
	1953	500	450	360
	1954	565	510	410

Ron Flockhart's Lister-Jaguar after his crash in the Argentine Grand Prix, 1957. Nobody was hurt

Left to right : Ron Flockhart, David Murray and Ninian Sanderson of Ecurie Ecosse receive the splendid painting by G. M. Turner of the famous 'No. 4' in the 1956 Le Mans race. The presentation was made by Mr. Eric Hardiman (*right*) on behalf of the Esso Petroleum Co. Ltd.

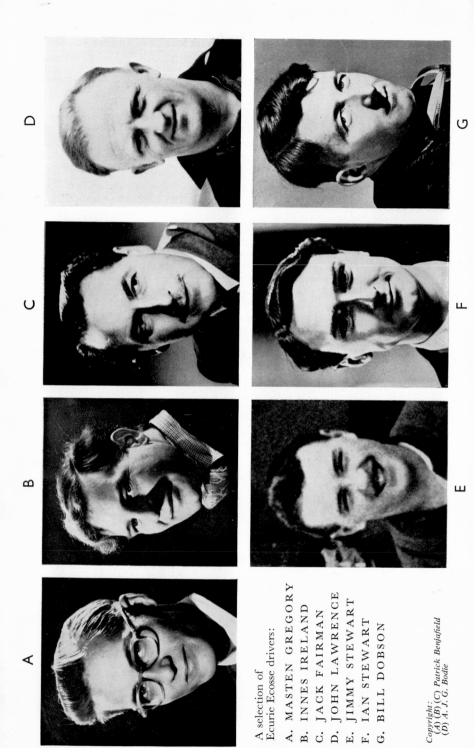

A selection of
Ecurie Ecosse drivers:

A. MASTEN GREGORY
B. INNES IRELAND
C. JACK FAIRMAN
D. JOHN LAWRENCE
E. JIMMY STEWART
F. IAN STEWART
G. BILL DOBSON

Model	Year	Measham Quotations in £		
		Class 1	Class 2	Class 3
Mk. VII M saloon	1954	635	570	455
	1955	705	635	510
	1956	815	735	590
	1957	950	855	685
Mk. VIII saloon	1956	1150	1035	830
	1957	1260	1135	910
	1958	1475	1325	*
Mk. VIII saloon Automatic	1956	1235	1110	890
	1957	1355	1220	975
	1958	1575	1415	*

(Mk. IX saloon, and the automatic transmission version too recent to give reliable used-car quotations)

Model	Year	Class 1	Class 2	Class 3
2·4 saloon special equip.	1955	975	875	700
	1956	1050	945	755
	1957	1200	1080	865
	1958	1375	1235	*
3·4 saloon	1957	1390	1250	1000
	1958	1525	1375	*
3·4 saloon automatic	1957	1450	1305	1045
	1958	1615	1455	*
XK120 tourer	1949	385	345	275
	1950	410	370	295
	1951	445	400	320
	1952	485	435	350
	1953	530	470	380
	1954	585	525	420
XK120 f.h. coupé	1953	580	520	415
	1954	645	580	465
XK120 d.h. coupé	1953	580	520	415
	1954	645	580	465
XK140 tourer	1954	760	685	550
	1955	820	740	590
	1956	920	830	665
	1957	1030	925	740
XK140 f.h. coupé	1954	795	715	570
	1955	855	770	615
	1956	960	865	690
	1957	1080	970	775

Model	Year	Measham Quotations in £		
		Class 1	Class 2	Class 3
XK140 d.h. coupé	1954	785	705	565
	1955	845	760	610
	1956	950	855	685
	1957	1070	965	770
XK150 d.h.				
Special equip.	1957	1495	1345	1075
	1958	1600	1440	*

Two facts which clearly emerge from these market valuations are (1) that the depreciation rate of all models of the Jaguar is on a very fair scale, and most models in the past ten years have held their price well. Also (2), there is a noticeable difference between Class 2 and Class 3, especially where a car is more than two or three years old.

A salient reason is that many people would prefer to buy a Jaguar that had been well maintained through the years, rather than attempt purchasing a 'bargain' in Class 3, where high cost of spares and specialist labour to overcome a major defect can be quite costly. For example, an XK140 tourer, 1956, has a quotation of £855, which is only £100 less than a similar car in Class 1 condition, or almost 'as new'. On the other hand, the listed figure for a similar car in Class 3 condition is only £685 at best, or £170 less than one in average condition. It is a question of personal preference, of course, if a motorist prefers to buy, say, an XK140 in good average condition, needing no immediate outlay on brakes, suspension, or a re-bore, or if a 'bargain' is preferred, leaving a cash margin of some £150–£170 to be spent on these essential repairs.

It should be borne in mind that there can be almost no limit when one sets about restoring a Class 3 car to bring it to Class 1. If a high milage has been covered, it is not merely a matter of a re-bore, or fitting new tyres, to make the car roadworthy. There will be an equivalent degree of wear in all moving parts—hubs, clutch, gearbox, electrical accessories and so forth.

That used Jaguars wear well and are a good buying proposition is confirmed by reports given in the technical Press. *The Autocar*, for example, has included two Jaguars in the

'Used Cars on the Road' series. A 1950 Mk. V saloon was tested in No. 133 of the series (7th November 1958), and a 1955 XK140 coupé was described and road-tested in No. 140 (10th April 1959).

The Jaguar Mk. V, registered in March 1950, had a recorded milage of only 6,425, but must in fact have covered very considerably more miles. Nevertheless, the tester remarked that 'its all-round condition is remarkable for an eight-year-old. Certainly it is well up among the best we have tried in the series, in terms of value for money.' What is even more remarkable is that under this strict test by *The Autocar*, the acceleration figures of the eight-year-old car were consistently better than those obtained with the model supplied new for test by Jaguar in July 1949.

Acceleration from 0–30 m.p.h. through the gears took 5·0 seconds, and 0–60 m.p.h. 17·6 seconds. The standing quarter mile took 21·4 seconds. Oil consumption was negligible, and an average fuel consumption of 16–19 m.p.g. was recorded. The tester commented that excessive pedal travel and the need for heavy pressures showed the brakes needed adjustment, that the steering was still light and accurate (Michelin X tyres were on the front, which in a car of this type might have been expected to produce slightly heavier steering), and that the car was good value for money.

The 1955 XK140 coupé, tested in April 1959, had covered 15,280 miles, but the tester was able to comment: 'The behaviour of this remarkable six-cylinder 3,442 c.c. long-stroke o.h.c. engine remains unimpaired . . . when the accelerator is pressed down hard there is again the familiar exciting change in its characteristics as, with something of a snarl from under the bonnet, the needle of the rev. counter surges round the dial, and the power builds up towards its potential 210 b.h.p. gross at 5,750 r.p.m. . . .'

It was found, moreover, that the 0–90 m.p.h. acceleration figure through the gears (26·7 sec.) was only four seconds more than when the XK140 model from the makers was tested new, in 1953.

Discussion with the service managers of a number of concerns handling used Jaguar cars—Merchiston Motors (Ecurie Ecosse), Duncan Hamilton, The Tourist Trophy Garage,

Longford Engineering, and others—together with personal experience prompts the suggestion that a number of minor mechanical features can profitably be checked when a used Jaguar is being vetted.

It is most important to get a signed warranty from the vendor with regard to the past history of the car, especially if it has been rallied or raced.

With all older types such as Mk. V and VII, examine the rear suspension, as after a very long period of hard use there is a natural tendency for rear-spring failures and—through neglect—of rusted shackles. The earlier $2\frac{1}{2}$- and $3\frac{1}{2}$-litre saloons, if in good hands, may have had periodic satisfactory spring attention all round, but the i.f.s. Mk. V was introduced in 1948, and from then on there was a natural tendency on the part of lazy owners to neglect the rear suspension. Incidentally, on the precise dating of these earlier cars, $5 \cdot 50 \times 18$ tyres were used on the earlier $2\frac{1}{2}$'s and $3\frac{1}{2}$'s, while the $6 \cdot 70 \times 16$ tyre was introduced in 1949. A small point, too, is that after August 1949 a simple rod-and-lever system was introduced to operate the bonnet catches, in place of cables.

With all XK engines it should be noted that the automatic choke has been arranged to cut out early, although of course the engine, if in good trim, should pull strongly a minute or two after a cold start. If for a considerable period the automatic choke has been adjusted on the 'hot' side, giving a rich mixture after the engine is really warmed up, there will have been unnecessary flooding of pistons and bores. This tends to dilute the film of oil so necessary, in the first minutes, to avoid unnecessary bore wear.

A slight gear whine in indirect ratios may not be a sign of any serious defect, but on a trial run it should be noted that a gear-crunch is not easily produced on a rapid change when the synchromesh is 'beaten'. Not only may this mean serious wear, in that the cones or dog-clutches are worn, but it indicates also a rather careless and ham-handed owner who has possibly not taken good care of other mechanical aspects of the car.

On the earlier Mk. VII and XK120 models four different types of gearbox may be found. The number of the box may be given on the scuttle plate, and is also stamped on a boss at the nearside rear of the gearbox itself.

First issue Mk. VII and XK120 had the SH and JH series boxes, while later models had SL or JL series. This is important to note when vetting a used model, as the two series, SH, JH, are not interchangeable with SL and JL. The SH and JH, also, are perfectly interchangeable as units, but many of the components are not. There are big differences between the SH–SL series, especially in the design of the constant pinion shaft and the countershaft gears.

The same feature should be noted with regard to rear axles of earlier XK120 and Mk. VII models. Two types were used, E.N.V. and Salisbury. Individual parts of these two different makes of axle are not interchangeable, although certain parts of each axle may be. In the Salisbury axle, however, it should be noted that the crown wheel and pinion for the two ratios available (3·77, standard, and 3·31, high) are not interchangeable.

Earlier Mk. VII's (chassis numbers around 710001, right-hand drive) were fitted with the Salisbury axle, and earlier XK120's (for example, chassis numbers 660001 tourer and 669001 f.h. coupé) may be found with either axle. The E.N.V. axle has its number stamped on the top of the differential nose-piece, while the Salisbury axle has the series number stamped on the gear-carrier housing.

For repairs of a used car fitted with either type of axle it should be noted that whereas the differential unit cannot be drawn out of the Salisbury-type axle, with the casing still fitted to the chassis, in the E.N.V. axle the differential unit is bolted to the axle casing, and is withdrawn forward. For rapid identification, no dipstick is fitted with the Salisbury axle, while the E.N.V.-type has a dipstick, and the filler plug is located at the top of the pinion-shaft housing. The Salisbury unit has the filler in the rear cover plate.

If either type of axle is replaced, or an axle of a different ratio fitted, the speedometer must be changed. The Smiths' code number, disclosing cable revolutions, will be found marked on the dial, thus: 'X 51691/28', signifying 1,225 per mile, suitable for the E.N.V. 3·64 axle, and X 51691/41, signifying 1,280 revolutions per mile, for the Salisbury 3·77-ratio axle.

A number of other points directly applicable to vetting a used Jaguar will be gleaned from Chapter 8. Earlier models of the 1½-litre and 2½- and 3½-litre may need minor modifications to lamps and reflectors to satisfy the statutory requirements under the Road Traffic Act, and as defined for compulsory vehicle testing. Publication No. 1762 has been introduced by Joseph Lucas Ltd. covering the modifications required regarding head- and sidelamps, reflectors, number-plate illumination and so forth. This can be obtained free of charge from any main Lucas agency. Other proprietary components such as carburetters are covered by makers' literature, also available in most cases free of charge.

S.U. carburetter adjustment is covered in the standard Jaguar manuals. With regard to earlier cars, however, the 1936 1½-litre Jaguar was fitted with Solex 35 FIL as standard, and the type 35 FAIE is a current replacement. The 1937 model had the type 30 FI which today can be replaced by the 30 FAI. Current Solex conversion for the 1938/39 and 1946/49 1½-litre Jaguar is the 35 HBFD, while on the 1937/38 2½-litre the current Solex conversion is a twin set of 30 AHG carburetters. Technical data leaflets on these models, as well as for others described in Chapter 8, may be obtained from any Solex agent, or from the Chief Service Engineer at the Solex Works, 223–231 Marylebone Road, London, N.W.1.

Lucas issue separate wiring-diagrams for various models. The standard owners' handbook includes an oiling chart but not a wiring diagram. The Dunlop Rubber Co. Ltd., Aircraft Division, Foleshill, Coventry, issue illustrated brochures detailing servicing procedure on disc brakes. Manual DM.1219 covers the Mk. I series as on earlier XK150's, and Manual DM.1213 covers the later Mk. II disc-brake installation.

Jaguar Service Manuals are available to all owners, and not only to the trade as is sometimes mistakenly supposed. They are very comprehensive publications, loose-leaf style, so are naturally costly. One of the most useful is the Service Manual for Mk. VII, VII-M and XK120 models, given in one complete manual issued at £3 18s. per copy. This can be obtained direct from Jaguars Cars Ltd., or from any Jaguar dealer or distributor on order. The smaller Operating, Maintenance and Service handbooks, as issued with each new Jaguar, are much less costly. The latest issue of the XK150 book, for example, is published by Jaguars at 5s. per copy.

Before checking any used car it is a good plan to purchase a copy of the appropriate Owners' Manual, so that the various servicing requirements can easily be studied. This should help in discovering any omissions in past servicing, which will of course affect the value of the car.

There is much to be said for purchasing a used Jaguar from a Jaguar dealer or distributor. It will be sold with a written statement of condition and guarantee, and for any servicing or replacements a Jaguar dealer is naturally in the best position to get spare-parts from the factory without delay. Sir William Lyons is justly proud of the feature he has helped to build for Jaguars, and which he describes as 'an aggressive sales policy backed by constantly intensified after-sales service', and it is this after-sales service which is important to the non-technical owner of a used car.

All enquiries to the Jaguar Company itself should be addressed to Jaguar Cars Ltd., Coventry (Coventry 62677), while individual component enquiries should go direct to Smith's Motor Accessories, the Dunlop Rubber Co. Ltd., Champion Sparking Plug Co. Ltd., S.U. Carburetter Co. Ltd., Joseph Lucas Ltd., Newton and Bennett Ltd., and so on. In London a special Jaguar Service Department is maintained by Henlys Ltd., where there is an expert staff of mechanics retained solely for Jaguar work. Enquiries should be addressed to Henlys Ltd., Jaguar Service Department, Great West Road, Brentford, Middlesex (Ealing 3477). It should be noted that direct issue of spare parts is not made from the Jaguar factory, and any parts needed must be ordered through the nearest Jaguar dealer or distributor. Jaguar part numbers are quoted in the large loose-leaf Service Manual, but not in the owners' handbook.

A great deal of help and instruction can be obtained through membership of the Jaguar Drivers' Club. As Sir William Lyons has explained: 'Formed by a band of enthusiastic Jaguar owners, the guiding principle of the club is that it is run by owners for owners, and although offically recognized by Jaguar Cars Ltd., it is completely independent of factory support for its existence and growth.'

The club, which is officially recognized by the R.A.C., has active branch centres in London and the Home Counties area, the Midlands and the North. It affords Jaguar owners the opportunity of competing in friendly rivalry with other Jaguar owners in various kinds of motoring events, and of competing against other makes in certain events. It keeps members up to date on all Jaguar sporting developments through news bulletins and the club magazine.

Full membership, available to Jaguar and S.S. owners only, entails a subscription of two guineas annually (life subscription £25), and there are also Family Membership and Associate Membership classes. The latter, restricted to five per cent of the total club membership, has the same annual subscription as full membership, and is designed for enthusiasts intending to become Jaguar owners in the near future. In each case application should be made to Mr. Eric G. Brown, Hon. Secretary, Jaguar Drivers' Club Ltd., 75 Baker Street, London, W.1.

Sir William Lyons is President, and Vice-Presidents of the club include Captain G. E. T. Eyston, O.B.E., M.C., and H.R.H. Prince Georg of Denmark.

Ten

JAGUAR SPECIFICATIONS

XK150

3½-litre XK engine, 83 mm. bore by 106 mm. stroke, fitted high-lift camshafts. 3,442 c.c. (210 cu. in.), compression ratio 8-to-1 (optional 7-to-1). Power output 210 b.h.p. at 5,500 r.p.m. 70-deg. twin o.h.c., driven by a two-stage roller chain. Twin S.U. carburetters. Cooling by pump and fan, with bypass thermostat control. Forced lubrication by submerged pump system incorporating a full-flow filter. Chrome iron cylinder block. Cylinder head of high-tensile aluminium alloy with hemispherical combustion chambers. Aluminium-alloy pistons. Steel connecting rods. Counter-weighted crankshaft 2¾-in. diameter, carried in seven large steel-backed bearings. Dual exhaust system. Four-speed single helical synchromesh manually operated gearbox with centrally positioned gear-lever. Ratios: 1st and reverse 11·95, 2nd 6·58, 3rd 4·54, 4th 3·54. Borg-Warner automatic transmission also available. Borg and Beck 10-in. single dry-plate clutch with hydraulic operation. Hardy-Spicer propeller shaft. Hypoid rear axle. Independent front suspension incorporating transverse wishbones and torsion bars controlled by telescopic shock-absorbers. Rear suspension by long silico-manganese steel half-elliptic springs controlled by telescopic shock-absorbers. Dunlop single pair pad disc brakes with servo-assistance. Central handbrake operating on rear wheels only. Rack-and-pinion steering, with 17-in. diameter steering wheel adjustable for reach. Turning circle 33 ft. Number of turns lock-to-lock, 2¾. Wire wheels with centre-lock hubs, Dunlop 6·00 × 16 Road Speed tyres. Large-capacity S.U. electric pump from a 14 imp. gal. tank. Lucas 12-volt electrical system. Twin 6-volt batteries, giving 64-amp. hr. at 10 hr. rate with current voltage control. Ventilated dynamo. Flush-fitting sidelamps and headlamps. Integral stop-tail lamps with built-in reflectors. Integral rear-number-plate lamp and reversing lamp. Flashing direction indicators with time-switch cancellation and warning lamp on facia panel. Panel light. Interior lights. Twin blended note horns. Twin-blade 2-speed self-parking screen wipers. Cigar lighter. Starter motor. Vacuum and centrifugal automatic ignition advance. Oil-coil ignition. Speedometer 5-in. diameter, and 5-in. diameter revolution counter. Ammeter. Oil pressure gauge and water temperature gauge. Fuel gauge with low-level warning light. Electric clock. Interior heater with windscreen demister. *Body* is aerodynamic two-door 2–3 seater, with two individually adjustable seats, with additional seating accommodation in rear for one adult or two children. All seats upholstered in finest quality leather, and leather-covered facia panel. One-piece wrap-round screen. Screen washers fitted. Screen rail leather-covered for passenger protection. Twin glove lockers in facia panel, etc. *Dimensions*: wheelbase 8 ft. 6 in. Track, front 4 ft. 3⅝ in., track rear 4 ft. 3⅝ in. Overall length 14 ft. 9 in. Overall width 5 ft. 4½ in. Overall height 4 ft. 7 in. Ground clearance 7⅛ in. Dry weight 27½ cwt.

Note: The recently introduced XK150 S has a specification basically the same as the stock XK150, but the XK engine in its 'Gold Top' form has the compression ratio stepped up to 9-to-1, and is fed by three S.U. carburetters instead of the normal two. The porting is also more streamlined. The XK150 S gives 250 b.h.p. at 5,500 r.p.m.

2·4 SALOON

Six-cylinder 2·4-litre twin o.h.c. engine, 83 mm. by 76·5 stroke, capacity 2,483 c.c. 112 b.h.p. at 5,750 r.p.m. Compression ratio 8–to–1. Twin Solex downdraught carburetters. Cooling by pump and fan, with bypass thermostat control. Borg and Beck 9-in. single dry-plate clutch with hydraulic operation. Four-speed synchro-mesh gearbox with central remote-control gear-change lever. Laycock overdrive operating on top gear only, or automatic transmission available. Gear ratios 1st and reverse 13·56, 2nd 7·96, 3rd 5·50, 4th 4·55, overdrive 3·54. Hardy-Spicer propeller shaft. Hypoid rear axle. Independent front suspension by semi-trailing wishbones and coil springs. Trailing link-type rear suspension by cantilever semi-elliptic springs and radius arms. Telescopic shock-absorbers at front and rear. Dunlop disc brackes, servo-assisted. Pull-up type handbrake mounted on floor of right-hand side of driver's seat. Burman recirculating ball-type steering with 17-in. diameter adjustable steering wheel. Fuel supplied by S.U. electric pump from 12 imp. gal. tank. Lucas 12-volt 51 a.h. battery. All-steel integral body-chassis construction. Four-door 5-seater body with leather upholstery, pile carpets and polished walnut woodwork. Interior heater and screen demisters and screen washers. Pressed steel bolt-on disc wheels with 6·40 × 15 in. Dunlop tyres. Easy-lift jacking system. Luggage accommodation 13½ cu. ft., with interior light. *Dimensions*: Wheelbase, 8 ft. 11¾ in. Track, front, 4 ft. 6⅝ in. Track, rear, 4 ft. 2⅛ in. Overall length, 15 ft. 0¾ in. Overall width, 5 ft. 6¾ in. Overall height, 4 ft. 9½ in. Turning circle, 33 ft. 6 in. Dry weight, 26½ cwt.

3·4 SALOON

Six-cylinder twin o.h.c. engine, 83 mm. by 106 mm. stroke, 3,442 c.c. Compression ratio 8-to-1. 210 b.h.p. Overhead valves operated by twin o.h.c. with high-lift cams. Twin HD6 S.U. carburetters with automatic starting carburetter. Cooling by pump and fan with bypass thermostat control. Borg-Warner automatic transmission with driver-controlled intermediate gear-hold. Ratios, direct 3·54, intermediate 5·08 to 10·95, low 8·16 to 17·6. Hardy-Spicer propeller shaft. Hypoid rear axle. Independent front suspension by semi-trailing wishbones and coil springs. Trailing link-type rear suspension by cantilever semi-elliptic springs and radius arms. Telescopic shock-absorbers at front and rear. Dunlop disc brakes with servo assistance. Pull-up type handbrake. Burman recirculating ball-type steering with 17-in. adjustable steering wheel. Fuel supplied by S.U. electric pump from 12 imp. gal. tank. Lucas 12-volt 51 a.h. battery. All-steel integral body-chassis construction. Four-door 5-seater body with leather upholstery, etc. Pressed steel wheels with 6·40 × 15 in. Dunlop Road Speed tyres. Easy-lift jacking system. *Dimensions*: wheelbase, 8 ft. 11¾ in. Track, front, 4 ft. 6⅝ in. Track, rear, 4 ft. 2⅛ in. Overall length, 15 ft. 0¾ in. Overall width, 5 ft. 6¾ in. Overall height, 4 ft. 9½ in. Turning circle, 33 ft. 6 in. Dry weight, 27½ cwt.

MK. IX SALOON

Six-cylinder 3·8-litre XK engine. 70-deg. twin o.h.c., high-lift, driven by two-stage roller chain. 87 mm. bore by 106 mm. stroke. 3,781 c.c., 220 b.h.p. Compression ratio 8-to-1. High-grade chrome iron cylinder block. Cooling by pump with bypass thermostat control. Cylinder head of high-tensile aluminium alloy with hemispherical combustion chambers developed from Jaguar C- and D-type racing heads. Aluminium alloy pistons and steel connecting rods. Forced lubrication throughout by submerged pump with full-flow filter. Twin S.U. type HD6 horizontal carburetters with electrically controlled automatic choke. Counterweighted crankshaft 2¾ in. diameter carried in seven large steel-backed precision bearings. Twin exhaust system. Straight plane steel box-section frame of immense strength. Torsional rigidity ensured by large-section cross members. Borg-Warner automatic transmission, with driver-controlled intermediate gear. Ratios: low-range 21·2 to 9·86, intermediate range 13·2 to 6·14, top (direct drive) 4·27–to–1. Hardy-Spicer propeller shaft. Hypoid rear axle. Independent front suspension incorporating transverse wishbones. Long torsion bars and telescopic shock-absorbers. Rear suspension by long silico-manganese steel half-elliptic springs controlled by telescopic shock-absorbers. Dunlop disc brakes with servo assistance featuring special quickly detachable pads (Mk. II). Burman power-assisted recirculating ball-type steering. Power-assistance is by hydraulic pressure from a pump driven from the rear of the dynamo. Number of turns lock-to-lock, 3½. Pressed steel bolt-on disc wheels with wide-base rims, fitted with Rimbellishers and Dunlop 6·70 × 16 in. Road Speed tyres. Twin S.U. electric fuel-pumps. Fuel capacity 17 imp. gal. tanks (two separate, of 9 and 8 gals.) with turn-over switch on instrument panel. Lucas 12-volt electrical system. Twin 6-volt batteries, giving 64 a.h. at the 10-hr. rate, with current-voltage control. Flush-fitting head and winglamps. Twin adjustable foglamps. Integral stop-tail lamps with built-in reflectors. Reverse lamp. Self-cancelling flashing direction indicators with warning light. Panel lights. Door-operated and manually controlled interior lights. Twin blended note horns. Twin-blade two-speed screen-wipers. Three cigar lighters. Starter motor. Vacuum and centrifugal automatic ignition advance. Oil coil ignition. Five-inch dia. 120 m.p.h. speedometer, and 5-in. dia. revolution counter. Ammeter. Oil pressure gauge. Water thermometer gauge. Fuel gauge. Electric clock. Screen washers. Built-in heater with controlled warm-air flow, and incorporating windscreen defroster. *Body*: All-steel full 5- or 6-seater, with sliding roof. Four doors. Ventilating windows front and rear. Special security locks to rear doors for child safety. Bench-type seat adjustable for reach. All seats upholstered in fine-grade soft-tan Vaumol leather over extra-deep moulded Dunlopillo. Polished figured-walnut instrument panel and interior garnishings. Two glove compartments. Passenger glove box with fitted lock. Sun visors. Four ash-trays. Polished figured-walnut flush-folding occasional tables in rear compartment. Padded armrests all round, and central fold-back armrests in front and rear compartments. Deep pile carpets upon ¼-in. felt underlay. Additional nylon floor rug in rear, boudoir clock and newspaper holder in rear compartment (bench-seat models only). Luggage locker fitted with interior light. Luggage space 17 cu. ft. A complete set of hand tools and small replacement items are carried in special flush-fitting compartments concealed in the front doors. *Dimensions*: Wheelbase, 10 ft. Track, front, 4 ft. 8½ in. Track, rear, 4 ft. 10 in. Overall length, 16 ft. 4½ in. Overall width, 6 ft. 1 in. Overall height, 5 ft. 3 in. Ground clearance, 7½ in. Turning circle, 36 ft. Dry weight, 35¼ cwt.

MK. VIII SALOON

Specification as for Mk. IX except for: Engine 3½ litre XK engine, 83 mm. bore by 106 mm. stroke, capacity, 3,442 c.c. developing 210 b.h.p. Laycock overdrive operating on top gear only, or automatic transmission available. Gear ratios: 1st and reverse 13·56. 2nd 7·96, 3rd 5·50, 4th 4·55, overdrive 3·54. Girling Dewandre vacuum servo-assisted brakes, self-adjusting hydraulic. Drum diameter 12 in. Friction lining area 179 sq. in. Handbrake lever flush between front seats. Burman recirculating ball-type steering, with 18-in. diameter adjustable steering wheel. Number of turns lock-to-lock, 4½. *Body* as for Mk. IX, bucket seats in front compartment, individually adjustable for height and reach.

The following two specifications are given for comparison :

XK140 SUPER SPORTS 2-SEATER

Engine, bore 83 mm. by 106 mm. stroke. 3,442 c.c. Compression ratio 8-to-1. Overhead valves by twin o.h.c. with high-lift cams. Twin 1¾-in. S.U. carburetters. Automatic starting carburetter and air silencer. S.U. electric fuel-pump. Water circulation by pump. 12-volt oil coil ignition. 64 a.h. battery. Ventilated dynamo. Single plate 10-in. Borg and Beck clutch. Rack-and-pinion steering. Four forward-speed synchro-mesh gearbox. Ratios: top 3·54, 3rd 4·28, 2nd 6·2, 1st 10·55. Central remote-control gear change. Hypoid final drive. Optional ratios available. Lockheed fully hydraulic brakes on all four wheels. Handbrake mechanical on rear wheels. Pressed steel bolt-on disc wheels with 6·00 × 16 in. Dunlop Road Speed tyres (wire wheels extra). *Dimensions*: Wheelbase, 8 ft. 6 in. Track, front. 4 ft. 3½ in. Track, rear, 4 ft. 2½ in. Overall length, 14 ft. 8 in. Overall width, 5 ft. 5½ in. Ground clearance, 7⅛ in. (On this model, as on the subsequent XK150, a convertible and also a fixed-head close-coupled 2/3 seater body was fitted.)

D-TYPE

Twin o.h.c. engine, 83 mm. bore and 106 mm. stroke. 3,442 c.c. 250 b.h.p. at 6,000 r.p.m. Compression ratio 9-to-1. Three twin-choke 45 DCO-3 Wever carburetters. Twin S.U. electric fuel-pumps. Water circulation by pump. Coil ignition. Borg and Beck triple-plate clutch. Four-speed all-synchromesh gearbox with central remote control change. Hypoid bevel rear axle with optional ratios. Integral body-chassis construction in magnesium alloy. Independent suspension of front wheels by twin wishbones and torsion bars. Rear suspension by trailing links and torsion bar. Dunlop disc brakes with servo assistance. Disc diameter, 12¾ in. Mechanically operated handbrake on rear wheels only. Rack-and-pinion steering, with 1¾ turns from lock-to-lock. Dunlop light alloy perforated disc wheels, with 3-ear centre-lock nuts. Dunlop racing tyres 6·50 × 16. Lucas 12-volt 40 a.h. battery with ventilated dynamo. 37 imp. gall. carried in two flexible tanks. Oil capacity 3½ galls. *Main dimensions*: Wheelbase, 7 ft. 6 in. Track, front, 4 ft. 2 in. Rear, 4 ft. Overall length, 12 ft. 10 in. Overall width, 5 ft. 5⅜ in. Overall height at scuttle 2 ft. 8 in. Turning circle, 32 ft.

BASIC LIST PRICES
(U.K. list prices without Purchase Tax, as at 1959)

	£		£
2·4	996	Mk. IX automatic	1,441
2·4 automatic	1,139	XK150 hardtop	1,175
2·4 special equip.	1,019	XK150 (Goldtop engine)	1,457
3·4	1,114	XK150 automatic	1,303
3·4 automatic	1,242	XK150 special equip.	1,292
Mk. VIII	1,219	XK150 convertible	1,195
Mk. VIII automatic	1,331	XK150 convertible	
Mk. IX	1,329	(Goldtop engine)	1,477

DATES OF MODELS

1½-litre

1,775 c.c. 4-cyl. 13·2 h.p. Reintroduced November 1945. Discontinued March 1949. Chassis Nos. from January 1948 onwards, 413030. In January 1949 standard saloon listed at £952 inc. P.T., and special equipment saloon £1,008.

2½-litre

2,663 c.c. 19·8 h.p. Reintroduced November 1945. In October 1948, Mk. V introduced with i.f.s. Drophead coupé also introduced in same month. Saloon discontinued, November 1949. Mk. V saloon discontinued May 1951. Drophead coupé discontinued July 1951. Correct Chassis Nos. Mk. V (Saloon) October 1950, 521500 on, and (Coupé) 540020 on.

3½-litre

3,485 c.c. 25 h.p. Reintroduced November 1945. Mk. V introduced October 1948, with i.f.s. August 1951, Mark V 3½-litre saloon and drophead coupé discontinued.

Mk. VII, etc.

October 1950. Mk. VII saloon introduced with XK120 3,442 c.c. engine, list price inc. P.T. £1,276. In January 1951 list price inc. tax £1,694. January 1954, Laycock de Normanville overdrive introduced as optional extra. October 1954, Mk. VII M-type saloon introduced, list price £1,680, increased to £1,779 inc. P.T. by January 1956. Chassis Nos. 722755 on. M-type Mk. VII saloon with automatic transmission introduced September 1955.

Mk. VIII introduced October 1956, with 3·5-litre engine. Listed at £1,897. Chassis

Nos. 760001 on. Mk. VIII introduced
October 1958, with 3·8-litre engine. Mk. IX
also introduced October 1958, with 3·8-litre
engine and disc brakes. Mk. IX saloon listed
£2,062 in 1958, with £53 extra for Reutter
seats.

XK MODELS AND DATES

XK120

Introduced September 1949, listed at £1,263
inc. P.T. Chassis Nos. 660001 on. Two-seater
sports tourer only. XK120 fixed-head coupé
announced 1951. XK120 convertible available
as from March 1953, listed at £1,644 inc.
P.T. XK120 discontinued October 1954.

XK140

Introduced October 1954. Chassis Nos. 661177
on. Listed at £1,598 for the two-seater and
£1,644 for the convertible. By October 1956,
d.h. and f.h. coupés both available with automatic transmission and/or special equipment.
XK140 discontinued February 1957.

XK150

Introduced May 1957 for export. Listed U.K.
£1,969 for d.h. coupé, inc. P.T. Available on
U.K. market as from October 1957. Overdrive
model available at £68 extra. XK150 Chassis
Nos. 827001 on.

INDEX

A

A.A.A., XK120 successes at initial meeting, 49

Abecassis (D.F.C.), George, and HWM-Jaguar, 58, 60 *et seq.*

Aerolite pistons, in XK engine, 40

Air vents, modification to front brake-drums, 68

Airline, S.S., development of car, 25

Alpine Trial, Talbot success in, 53

Arnott superchargers, Jaguar layout, 122

Arts, Royal Society of, 13

Ashcroft, I. Tim, and Lagonda Rapier engine design, 42

Austin, Lord, and Swallow Austin, 17

Automatic transmission, Borg-Warner, 96

B

Bailey, Claude, and XK engine development, 54

Band, Charles, and the Standard Motor Co. Ltd., 22

Barwell cylinder-head modifications, 120

Bentley, W. O., at Le Mans, 14, 30

Bentley Motors, and Jaguar team, 30, 44

Berry, R. E., and Jaguar Press relations, 29

Bira, B., races XK120, 48

Black, Sir John, and Standard Motor Co., 20 *et seq.*, 33

Boddy, W., and *Motor Sport* test of XK120, 43

Bolster, John, and *Autosport* tests, 63

Book of Motor Sport, 49, 59

Borg-Warner automatic transmission, 96 *et seq.*

Brown, Archie Scott, racing successes, 63

Bruce, Lord, and Ecurie Ecosse Association, 74

Buckley, Norman, water speed record with Jaguar engine, 15

Bueb, Ivor, 58, 64, 70, 73, 79

Burman, power-assisted steering, 102

Butler, H. J., and Dunlop disc-brake development, 75

C

Carburetter adjustment:
  for XK engine in general, 115
  Solex, 121
  S.U., 131

Camshaft drive for XK engine, 52

Clease, A. G. Douglas, and S.S.-1, 27

Clutch, Borg and Beck, 43

Collins, Peter, drives at Silverstone, 79

Costin, Frank, and Lister-Jaguar development, 63

Crankshaft:
  design in XK engine, 40
  regrinding, 119

C-type development, 57

Cylinder-block material, XK engine, 117

D

Daily Express Trophy, won by Peter Collins, 79

Davidge, A. V., and Swallow Austin, 19

Dewar Trophy, won by Jaguar, 54

Dewis, Norman, and second Jabbeke record, 48

Dick, Alick, and the Standard Motor Co., Ltd., 22

Disc brakes, 75 *et seq.*
  servicing, 80 *et seq.*